UNPLUG
FOR YOUR
MENTAL
HEALTH

Gabrielle West

Unplug For Your Mental Health

© 2023 Gabrielle West

ISBN 978-1-66789-864-3

eBook ISBN 978-1-66789-865-0

CHAPTERS

ACKNOWLEDGMENTS

To my amazing family and friends who are mentioned throughout the book, inspiring me to transform myself into who I am today, thank you for seeing the best in me.

CHAPTER 1:

INTRODUCTION–
TRUE SELF VS.
FALSE SELF

I never thought I was ugly per se, until I turned about thirteen. Everyone... and I mean **EVERYONE**; Let me bold it and type in all caps, in case there wasn't enough emphasis, goes through the uncontrollable metamorphosis that is braces, pimples and awkward bodies. Jason grew two feet taller during the summer of 5th grade going into 6ths, while Nick grew two feet wider because his parents worked full time and couldn't keep track of the amount of Cosmic Brownies and Mountain Dew's he consumed daily. We all went through it! Myself on the other hand, slicked my hair back in a low ponytail using just water to control my fly-aways, while wearing my older brother's navy-blue cargo pants that zipped off at the knees transitioning to shorts. SCORE. Got too hot playing kickball in gym? let's just unzip these babies and let the lower half of my legs breathe! No one made a single comment about my unique, yet functional style for a girl.... well, that I knew of, and I didn't even think twice about if they did. I was a weirdo, pre-teen trying to figure out what works for myself and what doesn't with my style. What was conventional and comfortable depending on how the day ahead was planned. Looking back now as a grown adult,

I complain to my mom "please tell me why you let me leave the house looking like that?!" shaking my head accompanied with a face palm. She simply replied, "because you wanted too!". Thinking, wow, she had no embarrassment watching her 13-year-old daughter strut around in an ankle length, jean trench coat and oversized Bobby Jack t-shirt venturing through the mall? Don't forget the Heelies! Honestly, she probably did feel the judgmental stares from passer-by moms questioning her parenting style, but through my eyes, nope! She was letting me do me and who was I hurting! There was no reason to question why I chose what I did and what it "meant" for me in the future, or even how it applied. Did it even correlate? I mean, they are just shirts and pants…why should she be concerned. She did try to reason and give a little guidance on what she thought would look better…. maybe a nice pair of jeans, hair bow, with a matching top. You know, the "norm" for an adolescent little girl dictated by style magazines and whatever was up and becoming that season. But my outfit for the day started and ended with me and those zip off pants. Why? Because I was the one wearing it? Of course! If I thought I looked cool, why did it matter how many others thought so, or didn't think so too. Or more so, why was it even being a topic of discussion?

Do you think if my mother tried to control what I wore back then as a kid, that it would have somehow morphed me into a better version of the adult I am today? If she threw those zip pants into the trash and forced me into a skirt and sparkles; Which would have been absurd to climb a tree in May I add, would it have determined how successful and or the path my life ultimately took? Now, being the same adventurous, but bleach blonde girly girl I have miraculously blossomed into, was there anything else that she expected or planned for me that would have altered my path or mindset if she had me focus more on my appearance? Did she know my weird style choices were just a phase of self-expression, or did she simply not care if they stuck around? If she would have been stricter on how she let me present myself to the world, would it have altered the person I am as a grown adult? Maybe of made me more successful in my career path, married and out of the house sooner, or even dictated the people I chose to hang out with? It all came down to the way she saw ME and her plan for my life, considering I didn't make the ultimate choice to be born...she did. Did that mean she had the underlying say over who I was and who I choose to grow into? Whether I fit into the social norms she wanted me to and what was acceptable at the time? All these questions of how I could have progressed into a better human being based off my mother and her parenting. And her ONLY. No one else had the jurisdiction to make a comment about who I was, that mattered anyway, other than the person who brought me into this world. If someone even looked at me sideways, mama bears' claws would extend from her firsts, and it would have been known to all who surrounds to not mess with her cub. I was protected, sheltered even by the acceptance my mother had for my individuality. No outside opinion mattered to my small brain because I would look back, notice my only form of guidance "approving" of who I was, and it was the only one that mattered to me. at that time. So, who and why is someone always dictating how an individual, young, or old should be now? Where they should be in life, whether it's an acceptable or unacceptable path and who gave the masses the power to dictate and add their two senses into the matter? if someone was falling behind progressing in the sociall "norms" for their age and what the criteria even looked like. No kids by age 30...OH LORD, stress, it's too late. WHO is dictating what a person should accomplish, look like, and over all status for a healthy life span and if it's being lived correctly? What is considered successful and unsuccessful, I guess it's not defined by being a kindhearted, genuine person anymore...but more along the basis of how successful and happy you perceive to be by others. Why now, is someone's appearance in question? They're house? How many vacations they take annually? The better you look to public, the better you're off in life! Right?! If you can convince them, you're winning! Whose opinions have we added to the mix to fluster over the way our children are being raised or how us adults live out our lives? What has changed so drastically that has parents trying to define their children's personalities, teens second guessing their appearance/self-worth, and adults thinking they are anything BUT successful in their current situation? Did something in our mental change as time progressed, along with all the technology advancements where we had to be more self-aware, to not stick out, or aggressively strive to not be different than what was shown through the media or the perfect norm. What was everyone else doing, wearing, saying as the new slang, and how can I fit in to display that I have it all together too! That everyone I surround myself has it all together! Aren't we exhausted yet trying to fit what we think now Is the perfect image?

When I grew up, meaning late 1990's into the early 2000's, there was no controversy of why kids wore what they did and how it would or would not alter their personality in the future. I mean, everyone had and still has their judgments, but the comments weren't as anxiety jerking as they seem to be now. No rule book on what an adolescent girl should or should not look like while running around playing outside or going to McDonald's for a birthday party. We all had bowl cuts and mullets for goodness's sake. No child was overly judged, meaning by adults and analyzed through every action or the way he or she played, because why did it matter? No random pop-up article on a popular social media platform alarming parent about the warning signs of being transgender because your daughter is going through a "tom-boy" stage and is wearing basketball shorts instead of a jean skirt. Which I played into and would have been confused as all heck if my mother tried to have a discussion with me over gender identity at age thirteen. Why pink is not a universal color and could alert the warning sings your son might be more emotional and potentially homosexual. There was just YOU and who YOU wanted to be while given the space and privacy to do so. Who created these articles and what was their purpose? It always loops back to this "who" I keep questioning, meaning the media. The words, "warning signs" strikes panic in the normal human, yet when it comes to raising a child, doing everything right is always on the agenda. Why where these articles created to strike fear in parents to worry about something as meaningless as clothing and or what they choose to play with. Why as humans, are we bringing attention to unnecessary and common personality traits that weren't an issue back in the day, like there isn't enough to worry about in the world already. Exposing this harsh judgment onto our children now that we "know what warning signs to look for" and being able to "fix" how our child progresses before its "too late" when all they crave is acceptance. Where did us humans, now in this technology fueled world, get the rubric of the ideal child. Who is creating this rule book of social norms and the warning signs that screams THIS IS NOT HOW YOU WANT YOUR CHILD TO TURN OUT? Yet here I am, a grown woman in my twenties comparing my true self back to how my mother allowed me to express my vision of what was cool and acceptable through something as harmless and style. What if she would have listened to other comments? Questioned me as a little seedling trying to grow my roots and figure out who I am? Alter who I am based on other people's opinions...as I question, it sounds more like our world today, scary.

So, if the only opinion I cared about most during my childhood (childhood meaning starting from birth until I entered the world of AOL Instant messenger at the early age of 10 years old), was my mothers, yet the teenagers now in this day and age are judged off every action depending on the hundreds of followers they entertain on multiple platforms, how is that altering our species mentally and should this really be the new norm society has created? How is this affecting the youths now as they are exposed to a world no generation has experienced yet, and what are the negative effects. There's this concept of 'true self' that was discovered by a psychoanalysis, which is a fancy term for someone who 'believes that all people possess unconscious thought, feelings, desires, and memories'[2] starting from an early age that just accumulate over time. Sometime between the 1940's into the 1960's the professor was able to scientifically map out and bring attention to different ways us humans react through our mental health being a real, genuine response compared to a fake, forced response. It took us as a species to venture past immaculate worldly disasters like WW1, The Great Depression, AND WW2, for someone to confirm basically the mental difference between a person being real and being fake, using relatable terms of today's day and age of course. How did it take that long and why?! You KNOW as well as I do, that back in the day humans were just as petty and judgmental over social status and appearance, just more on the sneaky and secretive end, not as out in the open. Out of sight, out of mind, right? How do you think the "fake laugh" or what we call our "customer service" voice was created? Responding how others assume we should for their benefit. For someone to write down the idea and provide a scientific study of how diverse and complicated our minds are wired, defining the difference between a true reaction and something forced made it an actual real thing to bring attention to, I guess. The man to be named D. W. Winnicott defined and coined the term "True Self" and explored the definition explaining it to be "a sense of self, based on spontaneous, authentic experience, a sense of "all-out personal aliveness," or "feeling real."[1] basically, stating that the concept is wrapped around everything that you truly are and what makes you and individual. So, I'm just spit-balling here, but if we are all created differently, having different reactions and thoughts that correlate with our upbringing and just how we are wired, why are we trying to create a perfect norm for the average human to follow?

Every age group has a set of accomplishments, social statures, and guidelines that needs to be completed and or shown off to present that you're doing it! You're getting through life successfully now! I remember my first year of high school, freshman year, I still hadn't received my first kiss. Thinking I should just get it over with; anxiety convincing me that I'm not enough. Clearly there's something wrong with me if not one single boy wanted to show they're lust for me physically. There wasn't pressure from my mom or my small inner circle of family members I respected and was use too, yet I felt like I was falling behind in some way making me question how my life was playing out…as if I had any control.

How embarrassing, I thought. Yet while on my Myspace (throwing it way back to the first social media most of these kiddos have no clue about, that I recklessly created without my mother's knowledge when 13 years old) I would post pictures, get those likes and attention I forever craved in person, to provide that little pep of serotonin release to get me by. I had this little escape to make me feel wanted at the very young age I was. Overly edited pictures with funky quotes, my favorite music video coded into my page, and specifically in order my "top friends" would start the virtual world that is social media and a peak into my world I lived. I would see "couples", I say that sarcastically as young relationships lasted a span of weeks, if serious, months and would post their awkward kissing pictures that I use to over romanticized in my brain (why lol). Thinking, wait how did they get together and why don't I have a boyfriend let alone my first kiss? Should I? Then one night, I received my first kiss unplanned. It just happened as if it was meant by the universe and the internal stress of questioning was gone, for a second. I can cross that off my life to-do list as a new teenager and onto the even worse anxiety of losing my virginity and when that's supposed to happen at an acceptable age deemed by society. A never-ending check list of social milestones I needed to get through to be successful for my age. I remember wanting to post a status. Trying to figure out how to let everyone know it happened, I was kissed without looking too eager or desperate. Like waving a flag, saying IM WANTED TOO! SEE! But I had a genuine need and want to be kissed, yet the anxiety that it should have happened sooner than it did, during the time was heart wrenching and took over so much of my mental capacity that when it did happen, I wasn't able to bask in what was supposed to be just my moment. It turned into something I needed to share. Playing it off daily, counting down until I was finally entering and passing through those stages of my adolescent romance acceptance like everyone does. A once in a lifetime experience and me wanting to make it known to the public and open then for judgment. I never thought as I grew up, that I would be subjected to or even now an expected timeline for when life milestones should happen. I kissed someone, it happened, and nothing changed mentally. Did it suppose too? Wasn't this what I've been waiting for and stressing so hard over? The expectations never matched the moment due to the immaculate buildup of stress and others input of what the moment should or shouldn't be. It went from my mother's opinion of me just seeking her acceptance, to the friends I surrounded myself with, multiplied by what I expressed of myself online. So many people were being allowed access into how I was progressing and experiencing things that even as milestones happened, I was still behind someone. Is that why my first kiss just seemed like a check point? Holly is celebrating her one-year anniversary with her boyfriend, while Stacey and her family went to Rome over the summer…and here I was. A small town, home bodied girl just receiving her first kiss as an accomplishment to start off my high school career. Making it seem so minute compared to what others were experiencing. How did they even compare? Of course, they didn't, yet I still felt so inadequate. Applying their input on my life as if I was going through mine correctly or incorrectly and how I saw myself comparing my journey to theirs. I was confused. I knew how I felt…. how my inner true self felt yet had to give the illusion my fake self-wanted to portray of yes, I made it! I'm right there with everyone my age! I'm doing great things too! Yet, still feeling so behind.

Has someone ever told you "Just be yourself!"? Prime example. It's exhausting trying to force your mental to react simply how it was not created to in a forced situation. Trying to be something you're not and it completely fails, to the point it exposes the hilarity of the action of pretending to be who you weren't formulated to be. Thinking, why did I even try to be that in the first place? That's the "fake self" or false ego reaction when you try to deny or alter your true self. It's kind of like holding back a sneeze, but it being too powerful to surpass. So, a weird noise is created by the compacted pressure of air from holding your nose. Its unnatural and goes against how the universe has formulated it to be! I loved this definition I came across, "False or "public" self appears polite and well-mannered and puts on a "show of being real." Internally, people who live out of their false self-feel empty, dead or "phony," unable to be spontaneous and alive, and to show their true self in any part of their lives."[3], so why in the world have we created this to be a social norm? Wasn't that explanation negative enough to try and stay away from? Maybe, to dictate the way we are perceived by others and for protection of our most vulnerable insecurities of being different.... ah! There it is. When we allow others into our world, we as humans are usually scared to show 'the messy' I call it. The raw, true rollercoaster of emotions that comes along with being human. I know I am and have completely and utterly accepted my flaws which a lot of people are taken back by. Social media has given us the tools to portray this false sense of a perfect version of yourself. Being able to post the BEST pictures (edited or not), witty status', or articles/meme's that correlate to who we want people to think we are, just so others may start to believe we are exactly that! You know, sharing a quote on Facebook that gives someone who just friended you a peak of your personality, your humor, or the way you spend your day. Allowing others an inside look of who you are (or want to be) and how you think, not showing the messy. Yet, we've forgotten we were created with so many flaws and that it's what makes us ultimately HUMAN. How do we know if a couple currently broke up? We check their profiles on all social platforms. Seeing if pictures are deleted, over analyze the things shared or the statuses posted. We have these timelines of life events that are shared to the masses when they use to be private. Whether good or bad. We seek more acceptance. Making it harder to cope or enjoy the moment, more opinions added to the situation, and heightened anxiety on how others are perceiving it in a positive or negative way. With so many people now in the audience, how can one not compare their life timeline to others and to think, what is the constant comparison doing to us as everyday people? Extending from all ages and genders mentally, if we feel others are progressing at a faster will we now forever be stuck in this foot race of "who appears more successful?". Others at the time experiencing more blessings when it's their season of change when you've been feeling stuck, leaving an emptiness of never amounting to the person you desire. We have this new surge of "influencers" and "social media famous" young adults who put content out in this virtual world to boost the use of the social networking sites. Something to grab the attention of the masses to flock more people to use the apps. More users, more revenue. Yet, the negative false self-image that everyone wants to show, has, in my opinion, changed the way we see ourselves. Adults, teens, children can create this perfect false sense of themselves that has made them lose touch with the real world, real emotion, and real-life connection. Losses seem harder, setbacks seem greater, the negatives that come with being alive feel too heavy as if no one else is going through anything of the sort. Social media my dear friends, is all an image of false self and we are FULLY submerged. Influenced by what we mindlessly scroll through altering our perception on what our own life should be. Not knowing the long-term consequences or the simpler life beyond the screen.

I'd like to take a little detour into my background as it explains so much into my writing style as this book will obtain a lot of what I've learned from past experiences into my newfound adult mindset. As I grew up in the surge of what is technology, being a millennial experiencing the impact of what has been social media. I know I have only mentioned my mother throughout my writing thus far as my father was not, how do I explain this effectively, I guess an active/positive role model in mine and my brother's childhood. More as that drunk, social butterfly that would show up at your school plays once every three years, even with 50/50 shared custody arrangement while projecting he was father of the year. He was loud, boastfully/temporarily proud, and occasionally sober. He knew how to play the game that is and was social media. Constantly posted pictures of his children at these events while providing an abusive and unstable home environment for half of our childhood lives. Showing off his normal family in the virtual world as if the local police weren't called every other weekend in the physical world. One time, he even went as far as stalking my eldest brother at his college football game to snipe pictures of his jersey while on the sidelines. Keep in mind they haven't had contact since he turned of legal age to escape the madness and was never invited nor involved with his football career. Falsifying facts and alerting the masses that his son's NFL season was right around the corner and how proud he was, without even having a relationship with his son. We were all confused and uncomfortable. He was obnoxious and seen in public persuading the masses of, "wow that's an awesome father!". Praise from outside friends and family of his parenting, yet there was nothing the people who knew the truth, could do about it. Just accept that one day it would catch up with him. What a manipulation of perception. He was able to convince others of this positive false self he created and continued to say what was needed to keep up with that persona. But as I quoted, a false ego doesn't and is not able to stick around long. As people started to question his made up narrative and ask more questions, the true self was always, sooner or later going to be exposed. Funny how the universe sorts out the imposter. Denying one's true self will always lead you back to where you started, with you. Continuing to try to convince others you're one way, when you know you're not leading you down a winding road of exhaustion to now where. Think if that time and energy was used for good. Acknowledging true accomplishments, improving relationships, and on his sobriety what my father could have accomplished. Yet, he wanted the positive benefits now that only the false image could give. Learning this at a young age opened my eyes to the negative reality that social media was. Exposing that there always was an underlying truth that only the people directly affected understood. That you're able to show and filter out what you did not want others to know to seem, better? Normal? Whatever the long strived for goal of acceptance was personally in your own brain. As my father was able to do. Opening my mind to the negative side of what "staying connected" with others through new technology entailed.

Denying one's true self only leads you back to where you started; the person you were formulated by the universe or God to be. It takes setbacks, failure of unachieved goals, and life changing events to figure out how we react and how we see the world, as we all react differently. Being pushed to our limits, unwillingly forced to react in whatever way we perceive best due to how our brain is wired. Our journeys are not comparable, yet that is our basis to a positive life span today. Show the good, follow your designed age/gender rubric and you'll be successful as we are told. But what about when the negatives emerge unwelcome, as they do for everyone. Being allowed to show the negative has its benefits as well as receiving the praise for the positives. As we start to see the expression of mental health, financial dismay, and broken relationships shared to whoever you've given permission to follow, it wasn't always the norm. As we start to see positive as well as negative self-expression the question remains as to why we even need to put our venture out there for the extra commentary at all? When did sharing everything that was meant for just you become the daily topic of discussion for the community? Positive or negative. What are we searching for through shared experience with temporary gratification of likes and comments? Do you ever think of how our parents and grandparents got married without changing their relationship status as a momentary check point? Or not sharing a long written out status of a "life update" as if an audience of people have been waiting for the next episode of what is the sequel of your life. What's crazy is no one knew any different back then. They just did what they wanted, celebrated events with the people it would directly affect, and went about their lives unbothered by the mass's opinions. Not basing success off the number of likes their wedding album received or the announcement of the gender of their first-born child. Expecting everyone who displays the "like" action virtually supporting your select shared life choices. I used to get excited when I had a reason to post. A new picture I looked good in, a renewal after a failed relationship. Whatever it maybe I loved these compiled memories that I would specifically organize on my page that showed everyone the person I wanted to be. What I wanted people to see when they creeped on my page, which pictures would pop up, the activist I support. All the things complied together to make up what is my profile. I, along with all the other users formed this page to basically define who were. Even if nothing like the person projected daily. Followers knew when you were sad by what you shared. They knew when you were falling in-love or heartbroken all from what we projected, while opening the door to judgment of your journey. To keep up, we post more. To show we aren't falling behind, we share more. As we try to keep up with what our lives should be, we lose who we are as this online self takes over. Creating fake social media personas all of what is not true and expecting a happy/ accomplished fulfilled life to follow to uphold this image you created. There shouldn't be check points/ to-do lists of what age we reach certain goals or don't reach certain goals as social media enforces.

Social media, for me starting at the influential age of 14 as I mentioned above, has opened that portal to allow us humans to compare, leaving us feel underwhelmed with where we've been and done thus far. How much of my life I've compared to others considering that's all I've known? How long I've felt less than because of my social, financial, and marital status when the only opinion that should matter is mine, and the circle that surrounds my life. I've decided to unplug which sparked the momentum for me to write. I deactivated all socials, no longer even searchable on google, other than my Snapchat. As I did filter and delete all who didn't interact with me in the last year and still wanted to feel somewhat connected. I would always flirt with idea, but finally became so low mentally with where I was in my life, that I was able to connect it to the false self I was trying so hard to portray to everyone else while crying behind the screen about where I was status wise. How I progressed career wise, how I look nothing like I did in high school (even the year before) and how I was progressing romantically all judged by people who had no direct correlation with me and who I was as a person. I didn't want anyone to "creep" on my profiles as I didn't feel like that is or who I truly was…and experienced the thought to myself, did I even know who that is? Considering the person, I displayed was altered by how the world displayed I was supposed to be online. All the opinions and guidelines I suddenly gave no voice as I stepped back. Experiencing this self-exploration journey, unplugging from the virtual me I created to find MY true self. 100% aware of the world and the little experiences around me that made me feel alive and that would morph me. That made me feel human and comfortable with who I am. As you read, I hope to inspire you to experience all that is your life without being afraid if you're living it correctly despite who does or doesn't think so online.

CHAPTER 2:

NOT EDITING
WHO YOU ARE

Being able to look back on our accumulating memories over a span of time to see where we were in the last years of our lives and acknowledge the change to our surrounding life has always been a love hate relationship for me. Having a Timehop or Snapchat memory notify you of the media stored from that same exact day, the moment it was able to reconcile the data from however many years ago. Some sad, some happy. Some making me see how much I lived and where I use to be, creating that whimper of what once was. As I see my face in these pictures and videos, I'm able to recollect how I was feeling at the same time and place it was taken. What was going on that day and mentally if it was positive or negative along with the people who were active in my life during that time. It left a trace of that small memory and scenario once lived. Social media has gifted us this new feature to look back on memories and the ability to leave a path of accomplishments and details that we may have forgotten as time passed if left undocumented. At the end of our roads, when our time here on this planet must come to an end as everyone's does, there's that something of you left behind. All these usernames, emails, and accounts designed by you that will keep close ones connected with our once alive spirit through these memories and experiences stored. People will be able to remember us how we were, how we laughed, and at the same time form all the data together to create a reel of what once was our lives how we saw through our eyes. The moment you showed your grandma what filters were for the first time, the family picnic where your brother spilt his plate of lasagna on the kitchen floor, or even the people who were apart of these small snippets of time in your life all compiled into a cluster of beloved moments of the past. Is that what is going to define us when we go or even defines us now? Is that something we are hoping for; to keep these memories and videos so we have some sort of mark left of the life we once lived? Who we are and how others were able to experience us being a part of their life? Yet, we have only showed what we believed made an impact and were able to leave out the things that didn't. It's not like we are able to download what was behind the mask of the screen recording. You didn't record the time you embarrassed yourself while too drunk at the family party or even when you got fired from your first job. There's no way all the moments and feelings you've had were able to be documented to reveille the answers you are looking for, who was/am I, how was I perceived to/by others, or lastly be remembered as a whole? Will taking these videos and keeping them or memory provide comfort or be just a cluster of extra data that will be deleted someday. Who are we taking these videos for and what is the lasting impression they will have? Are they more for us or other people? Frantic open-ended questions that we all want answered. But the idea of it all is to stop and take a breath. Realize, that these are moments of your life you thought were worth documenting. No one else views them the same way as you do or did as it was happening. You remember the emotions connected, how you felt during that time and you're able to physically collet these memories for you to remember forever on this minute divorce that we give so much power to. Making these moments feel important, above average enough to be shown or kept. As if life wasn't already.

Before social media there was no way to capture all these little moments. No effortless app on a handheld, travel sized devise that made it so easy to store. It was just you compiling these experience and feelings connected to you somewhere in your brain to reminisce on. As we continue to want to film everything that happens in our lives, it becomes a relay of what we found convent enough to film, not necessarily based on importance. Just because it wasn't recorded, doesn't meant it didn't make an impact or was a memory worth keeping. Yes, we like to show off our experiences, keep track of where we've been, and hopefully pass along our memory as we pass through time, but each recording I believe is a cluster of experiences you want to hold onto as time moves forward just for you specifically. We want to remember the good, the fun, the people that made these times of our lives so special, as we all know they are temporary. Which is why I believe we stress to capture the moment before it passes. I mean, why do we always record the 4th of July firework show? You know you will never go back and re-watch the videos taken. Yet, at the time it's something momentous and worth sharing. We scramble to capture the moment to remember and have it if our life permits, remembering what once was. Being able to reminisce on the good, which can misconstrue our journey. Leaving a distorted path of moments that display what was able to be saved. Losing the whole story. Forgetting details that happened of that specific day and time and altering memories of how we've grown from past trials and tribulations. Editing and cropping the whole story only remembering it the way we want, not the way it was. Including the positive and negative of any life experience, like I said only now becoming more of a norm to expose has become a necessity to be true to who you are as a person. As a society we love to be perceived as something positive, but as we're able to show and remember both sides hopefully the whole story now we can uncover the realness of being human and being the true you. Remembering the hardships and struggles it took to achieve the moments of pure bliss. All smiles and different experiences we wanted to pinpoint leaving out what came and went too fast to record, along with the messy that we didn't want to remember. Being able to reminisce on the whole truth of you. As technology progresses, is it whatever that is left on our devises that ultimately defines our time here spent, right? I mean, it is the person behind the phone that is the core driven source to find sole purpose of these irreplaceable memories. No one else thinks the video of your dog running in his sleep as a puppy is as cute as you do, because just you lived it and had an emotional attachment to the memory. But all these compiled saved moments in time can help guide you through and indefinitely define your true self and how you ended up reaching where you are today. Like a map. Narrowing down your life experiences along with where you been, who've you done what with, and where you end up. But will these complied memories be something we can truly rely on to tell us who we are if we haven't captured everything?

I'm able to admit that I feel lost a lot of the time with the direction my life is headed, as any normal twenty something girl would. When I feel inadequate from the lack of accomplishments within the last few months or so, I'm able to take mental inventory through all the media I happened to save. I'm able to track my weight loss…or gain. I'm able to see even the small details I might have overlooked that would alter my indefinite future. Projecting comfort from the saying "I'm not where I want to be, but I'm not where I use to be" as I'm able to piece together amazing moments I've been able to capture to push me along to the next adventure. Without this tool, how would I have been able to remember all the details, or most of the journey which led me to where I'm at today. There's positivity behind just capturing what you want. A timeline of events that makes you stop and realize the venture. Then I wonder, how did our parents remember theirs before the constant notifications of memories. Or were these snippets of time captured just simply that, a thing of the past meant to be left. Something that came and went, embraced to the fullest knowing there was no convent way to save the moment like we have now. No comparison of one's journey to another or even comparable to your own journey of where you were before, just embracing what was and letting it go. No rushing to get the camera in an exciting moment; just being able to be present a live it. There was no devise to relay back to that was able to compile all the memories, details, or demographics of your life during that time. A simpler form of life basically soaking in all the moment had to offer and letting it be just that. Not being able to reflect leaving room for eagerness into what's to come next. Rather than looking back on what was. All the things you stressed to record for memory, leaving your brain just focused on those in the past rather than the possibility of the future. Our parents, before phones just lived with small traces of pictures taken every so often; family reunions, birthday parties maybe, even holidays just too look back on to remember what once was, unlike our generation comparing experience to experience daily. It's weird to think that one day my children will be looking at my camera roll on my phone instead of a photo album complied of my lifelong memories. Instead, millions of moments of my life captured by a devise I gave the attention to hold my journey. Are we going to store our SD cards away in the family chest in the basement, to let future generations cherish in place of the boxes and boxes of printables and VCR tapes? Weird to think that could be the way of the future. They will never know of most of the hardships we had to deal with, seeing as our life looked so great and full love and happiness. What hard decisions we had to endure, the struggles to make ends meet or to be able to put food on the table. Who would want to document that? As that maybe, we aren't setting the right tone for how our lives were lived and how it's not all rainbows and butterflies. Why do we only keep the positive to shut out what negative we might have felt and is it right to tease our future selves into thinking the moment was better than what it was? Seeing as people discouraged themselves now comparing our experiences to another, will future generations look back on our time and expect we had it made in the sun? Unless we start to show what's true, as I know social media isn't going anywhere anytime soon, the fake self will continue to take over to continuously make us miss the past or even compare the current. Leaving the trace of the false ego we are wanting so badly to perceive to be. Leading further and further away to exposing who you are and how to live your life through just that. You. Not just an image or username. Whether we decide to start to show the real 100% of the time and not just when acceptable, or remove ourselves virtually for good, there must be a way to disconnect this way of thinking of upholding specific standards. We can't edit our lives to show only half of the battle.

I'm guilty of it; deleting what I don't want to remember. The awkward, crazy, embarrassing moments once captured. Seeing an "ugly" natural picture of me and begging someone not to post for all their followers to view. Stressing dramatically for others not to see that undeniably real side of me. The natural, normal side where I can look unattractive, unappealing, and downright not even like myself. It depends on the angle; we've all heard that! You know, like when you accidentally open your front facing camera and it exposes your three chins and the glorious resting mean mug, we all have. I have the image of myself that I try to portray, you know the one I described earlier through our online fake selves that I must uphold. The ego I keep and will continue to keep mentioning until the reality of how FAKE it is sinking in. The social suicide of my crush seeing a bad picture of me was detrimental to my social life. I remember I use to comment under pictures I thought were so terrible, stating "that's not me? who is that?" (lol) I'm also guilty of posting a bad picture of someone else that I believed I looked good in for self-virtual gain! There are two sides to that game everyone online played, and it has defined our new culture that involves social networking as the new way of life. So many new terms and dangers to look out for whether it be the anxiety of comparison, cat fishing, or the social depression of not amounting to what others happen to be experiencing. So much more can be hidden while shielding behind a screen accompanied by added secret stressors that have not yet been brought to light as everything looked so pristine and proper with added help from our keen eye of filtering out the negative.

As memories happened and pictures started to accompany these events, we had to post! Showing that I have this entertaining life, am attractive, and people want to be around me! Like hello, look how great I look! When literally none of the people I posted for online, my what, 600+ followers on Instagram had anything to do with my life now, nor cared specifically about me and my life directly. It's all an image, remember? Yet I continued to post to uphold my virtual reputation! My followers not seeing that I'm having a great night out of drinking, the term "snap it or did it happen?" was like gospel for me proving I am fun and can experience fun events. It's like we couldn't live without others knowing what we're doing. If we could convince them our lives are cool, wouldn't we think so too? Yet, how overly edited and filtered can we admit the ugly was taken out and how much we are deleting from what others viewed. By making the profiles, we've allowed them a small look into our lives, but as we became more active, we were able to dictate the side of us that were shown. What could have been perceived of an amazing night out at the club could be two girls sitting in a dive bar with just them and the bartender. First date with someone new to make an ex jealous, when it's really you and your dad cheers-ing your glasses together at the kitchen table. There are so many manipulations of perspective, along with being able not to show the bad that can convince others this person you're trying to be, it's not so much the truth. Today, we're all so wrapped up in showing off who we hope others see us as, that our inner selves are dying to be taken care of. There's only so much we can brush off. So much we can't show until the universe decides to expose it for you. I mean, prime example, every celebrity. They look perfectly fine until one day they have a mental break down, decide to shave their heads or end up in rehab. There's only so much disguising who you are can do. Whether we delete or try to hide others from our ugly, run from our past or problems, or make others view us in a different light, social media has given us some tools to be able to control some aspects, but not from who matter.

At the peak of social media, I'd say I was in my late teens. I'm meaning Twitter, Facebook, Instagram, and Snapchat all new, all coming with their own anxieties and the platforms flowing full force into my teen to adult development. I received all my news, latest drama, information from these platforms and continuously cycled through them all for entertainment and pleasure. Closing one and opening one rapidly in a repetitive cycle on my new iPod touch as smart phones were still a thing of the future. Exposing the internet to my teenage content not knowing the dangers nor the addiction of wanting to feel connected or heard. Close one, open another on a constant, repetitive cycle seeing if there were any updates. All it took was one like on a post, tweet, or status and I craved more. Seeing as I added my new crush, knowing he's lurking and swiping past my content made it even more exhilarating. I was open and accessible to all who wanted to follow. Hoping it would catch his eye, or anyone's for that matter and somehow lure them my way. Hundreds of people lurking in the virtual shadows. Some I knew, a lot I just added/accepted for the follow. How crazy I let these randoms into my life, posting about my school, work, or vacations allowing this information available for God knows what or who. You know, the goal was to always have more followers than you're following. Defining your worth and social status in numbers.

Looking back on my Twitter feed that I started my last year of high school and ending the constant updating my first year of college, wondering why I put this information out into the world and who cared to accumulate it. Talking about break ups, feeling alone, insecurities, hoping for a like and for someone to reach out to validate. It's like I turned to this temporary comfort in hopes it would lead to true change in the physical world. Waiting for the right person to see it, send me message, fix what I was anxious about. Putting it out there made me feel what I thought was better, even with no reply. I finally made the ultimate decision to delete is as why would anyone want to relive the mind of a 18/19-year-old girl going thru the struggles of thinking their old enough to take on the world yet needing their mother to schedule their doctors' appointments. I finally reread what I made available to the world when it should have been in the security of a diary. Basically, all this information was compiled up over years and who or what saved this content is beyond me, yet I was the one who put it out there, so it was free game. Exposed, open, and available for whoever, anytime unfiltered.

People had access to how I felt in any split moment of time and able to make assumptions about me as a person, extreme or not because of my uneducated brain making the content more than available through

Twitter. My beliefs and views shared, my thoughts on the latest fad and relationships I had. Allowing a virtual timeline of events that happened in my life, exposing my insecurities in the split second not knowing how I was being perceived or even second guessing if it should be put out there for everyone to see. Obviously, I had not known the pleasure of privacy. So instead of one platform being able to edit out the bad of the physical self like Instagram, which was made for photos, this platform was a wide-open look into what was my teenage psyche, and it was wayyyyyy too much shared. Embarrassing even as my adult self was able to read back before deactivating. There was no one monitoring my adolescent brain from filtering out what should be expose and what didn't. I needed a mental sifter for the thoughts I had and a lot of what was posted out of haste that got me in trouble. We were the first generation who grew up with access to this virtual word, like my mom knew what I was posting. She had no idea what a Tweet was, even with a detailed explanation. Now, the thought of letting a child loose on the internet sparks hazard. There are specific apps even filtered for children, considering we learned from trial and error from my generation. The rules and dangers weren't exposed yet as the understanding of this new social world by the normal family was few. It wasn't all about sharing too much, rather than posting things you know would appease the masses or attract the most attention. Glad I deleted the feed as readers can't go back and reread how dramatic I was, saved myself further shame. Getting to the point that all these platforms had a different agenda. A way for you to connect with, love coming back to use, and sharing your information or thoughts for entertainment. Which it was! It was exciting connecting with others, knowing you aren't alone, and that any moment another interaction could happen. Posting something risky to attract whoever, but it's all for the attention seeking whether good or bad. Stirring the pot as I like to put it. Putting a side of ourselves out there, a peak into our personalities, our minds, or our everyday opened the door for others to enter and reply. As the audience grew the greater the reward….and the bigger the downfall. Which wasn't recognized until the faults happened.

We kept making ourselves accessible trying to control how others viewed us in this different world. Exposing too much at a certain time, having to do damage control. Learning what's too much and not enough. Limitations and status' that get more attention and the reaction that we're looking for. Editing out the bad, highlighting the best, creating this perfect version of who we are and being able to share this person who never did wrong with the world! Then we step away, eager to return. Not being able to edit the normal worldly negatives that pelage ALL our lives that we try to hide.

The most serious relationship I was in lasted a LONG two years and was one of the most mentally abusive, controlled partnerships I think anyone can endure. Now looking back of course, not seeing it at the time. He cheated, not once, but twice. Me finding out by the other females finding my information through social media. Not the point, but the reason I stayed with him is because the image I portrayed and what I wanted it to be so badly. Not coming to realization of what it was. A waste of time and love. He ended up buying me a house (later used as a tool to control me), getting my name tattooed on him (then covered up), and buying everything my eye sparkled at while out shopping (which all ended up in the trash). There was a moment that I returned to a small grocery store in my hometown while still in this relationship. I used to work there on my time off from school, no more than 10 isles and a total of 5 employees working at a time. An older woman who I use to work with said in exclamation as she hadn't seen me in a while, "Gabrielle you look so happy with who you're with! He looks like a keeper! That makes me so happy for you!!" And my face dropped. I tried to reply, put on the fake smile I portray online, but knowing how miserable I was on the inside I just nodded and continued to search through to store to get what I needed. Disregarding her comment. Usually, I was able to brush those comments off and agree like the statement was true, but this time was different. I realized I accomplished what I wanted. I fooled everyone into think I had it all. I'm so happy and finally have the boyfriend, house, and dog… My little family. Yet I was lost and dying on the inside. Crying every night because he was so cold. Feeling alone as he pushed me away and all I wanted to do was please, loosing myself in the process. I was just convincing everyone else of how in-love I was when I for sure wasn't. Making sure to post pictures from our multiple Disney trips a year with his family. When little did everyone know, he would yell at me in front of Cinderella's castle right after the flash of the camera and fake smile. Endless pictures of us together, forcing him on adventures he didn't want to be on, complaining as to why I needed to capture so many moments. Snipe as many smiling pictures as I could, just to post and fool like I had what everyone wanted. I lived a life full of negativity yet online I was able to only show what I wanted, tricking everyone but myself. But one day of course it all had to fall apart as I couldn't uphold the fake image any longer. I finally broke and had to leave to find myself once as again as I faked who I was for years. Pushing the do-over button learning, the truth always comes out as the fake self exposes.

The virtual world we are all so addicted too can't capture what has formed us into the humans we are today, which includes the bad, ugly, and messy. We allow people to make judgements off what we show, allowing them to believe they know who the true us is. Endless accessibility with such an audience of viewers casting their judgments on our lives has added more pressure than I think we have realized. Starting from when I was the young age of fourteen venturing into my mid-twenties, that's 10+ years of being completely plugged into this other world that was able to define me. I know I'm not the only one who has felt this constant tug of your online self-compared to in person.

This is how everyone one my age grew up (Millennials), excited for the new advantages but unaware of the affect it has on our mental health. Only learning from experience and getting fed up with the constant pressure to uphold myself. Statistics show from the years 1999 – 2018, the late nineties to around a peak year for social media, the various "age suicide rate among females increased 55%, from 4.0 in 1999 to 6.2 in 2018, while the rate for males increased 28%, from 17.8 to 22.8."[4] and has been on a constant "2% rise per year from 2006-2018"[4] and growing. Now, I'm no scientist, but there must be something causing this constant growth. This change in the way we think has been altered as a species. It's not one group; it's all races, ages, shapes, and sizes that are affected soiling our minds with something that is plummeting our mental health. The hypothesis I have created, and I think others can agree that as technology advances, as wonderful as it is to keep people connected, has put pressures on our wellbeing/growth to succeed and play into what is the successful life. Which, by our standard is HARD AS HELL to achieve, if anyone really has? We clearly are all in the same boat. If suicide rates for all are on a continuous rise, why aren't we all pausing to try to find the source? There's no way to edit out the bad in real life, making it difficult to accept when it happens. It's inevitable! But the world is showing this impossible vision on perfection and when not reached, utter failure floods the mind. Feeling like no one else is experiencing setbacks and its almost embarrassing now to admit. There's a way to stop the downward spiral of your mental health…. simply unplug. Let's stop the comparing and creeping. Let's stop traveling just to be able to take cute pictures to post. Let's stop inviting people to make their own judgments about or every day and be able to sit with who you are and the people who surround you. Stop trying to impress the masses when you and who you surround yourself with are the ONLY ones who matter. You choose what to put your energy into, its time it be your true self on and offline.

CHAPTER 3:

WHO ARE YOU BEHIND THE SCREEN?

Great question. How do we even answer such a complex question that could have so many answers? At that, do we even know who we are considering we are forever changing due to circumstance. There's three main psychological point of views that have narrowed down the perception of ourselves and how to determine an answer for this inquisitive question. First off, how to define who you are initially comes from how you view yourself. Duh. What you think your greatest assets are, how you treat people, and the overall image of who you want to be. It's complied of every life experience and impactful moment that has shaped your way of thinking. Your learned traits, reactions, and emotions all connected to this internal magnet that collects all this data and forms what is perceived to be specifically you! The hard part about this concept is if the person the world has formed you into, is something that is positive or negative in your judgement. Whether you like yourself or not. You're over all self-worth banks off this idea and generally forms your outlook on your entire existence. Explains why self-love is so important. If we don't happen to like the person looking back at us in the mirror, how do we expect others to as well? As stated by the Cleveland Clinic, as individuals "we continually take in information and evaluate ourselves in several areas, such as physical appearance (How do I look?), performance (How am I doing?), and relationships (How important am I?)"[5]. If we tend to have more positive answers to these simple questions then obviously you tend to live a very optimistic, glass half full life. You see yourself in all aspects and make the decision that you like the person you are and can live out subjectively. Now, on the opposite side, obviously if the responses to these questions tend to be negative, your life will follow that path into what is dark and twisty. Leading your mind, nowhere but a dead end of depressing thoughts about yourself. Take a moment and answer those questions in your head. Evaluate where you are and allow yourself to get a full grasp on how you view yourself to make the judgment of what self-image you portray. Let's start there.

Now that you have a better understanding of the first concept, you can better judge how to improve your view of yourself and the part you play in the world. What aspects you need to pay more attention too and the others you are content with. If your answers don't specifically lean one way or the other, then that still means there's room for improvement! Starting from the first question asked, whether it's how you view your body image or over all appearance. There are many ways you can alter appearance but healthily only doing it for yourself! Remember, we're not here to fit into societies norm or the medias idea of beautiful. This goes off what makes you feel comfortable in your skin at the end of the day and improving yourself, for yourself. Being alive gives us a free pass to express our individuality as we please, which differs from person to person. Be able to envision the best version of yourself (if you don't think you've accomplished that already) and then take action to manifest it! It's as simple as wearing more jewelry or putting on lips stick that will break the anxiety caused rut that allowed you to stay stagnant in your butterfly transformation! One small change will alter your mindset and allow you to take the first small steps to who you see as your best self. Starting that positive chain reaction into self-acceptance.

Second line in question as follows, how am I doing? Doing in what? Well…EVERYTHING! How much effort are you entering in your everyday? Are you putting your best foot forward or continuing the same old and still complaining? Are you striving for your career of choice or staying in a place out of convenience? Your circumstances play a big role in yourself view but also being able to create the best outcome while only stressing about what you can change is the hard balance. Understanding that you are not what is happening, yet the way you respond determines the outcome. How you respect/interact with others, spend your day, and whether you strive to keep pushing forward. How you "do" in all areas reflect greatly on your personality and over all person you are. If you don't like the outcome, try to respond different. Waking up every morning and dreading work isn't going to change the situation, instead, tell yourself something great will happen today! Watch your world view change. Starting a chain of positive interactions or reactions to situations can kick start something great in anyone. So, think, how are we able to do better? Even if you already answered positively, we know no one is perfect. We may have come a long way from where we were, but there's always more to grow as I stated we are forever changing.

Lastly the question of importance. Remember, we are talking how YOU see yourself. How important is the role you play in your day to day? Are you taking initiative to improve your own circumstance and be the change you want to see, or are you standing idly by hoping for a new outcome? There are many ways to show yourself that you are important. Taking time out of your day to collect your thoughts or actively do something that makes you happy! Showing yourself that you're a part of this planet and that you can make an impact leaving you feeling involved, useful, needed. Striving to be better for yourself and the ones around you. A lot of people get lost in this idea, that the meaning to their life has simply escaped them. This has a lot to do with this same concept. Not feeling important or needed is a human necessity and when there happens to be low points, we tend to sulk. Keeping a reminder and telling yourself that you are important on a daily with help keep that train rolling! As emotions fluctuate, I am also an offender of this same practice I'm preaching, it's natural to question your worth. But if you continue to recognize its happening and are still able to grow from the negativity, then you're winning!

By asking yourself these questions and diving into positive responses hopefully being able to lead you toward a healthier view of the person you are. Keeping these solutions in the back or your mind will be able to help transform who you see yourself as and lead you toward living a full life you love. Seeing yourself positively is the first step to a happy life considering if you don't believe it, who else will. Let's work on unwiring the negative thoughts and positively affirming why we are the way we are, beveling in ourselves, and then being able to watch the good follow.

Second point of view happens to be the exact opposite. Not how you view yourself, but how you think you are perceived by others. The perception of self-consciousness and the either confident or reluctant side that exposes itself when out in the public. The source that is social anxiety that I know all too well. Thinking how others are judging you and how you are affected by the possible scrutiny. While on the other side, noticing others checking you out driven by pure attraction. Noticing someone noticing you and the either nervous sweats that set in or the enlightened stride you get acknowledging the appreciation. Or you can simply not care! Either way, this perception is fueled by how you view yourself to start and if the opinion of others has great effect on you. Whether you are content with who you are including the positive or negative judgement of others.

Growing up in a public school it was hard to ignore the comments of others. I felt like the "mean girl" opinions stuck my nerves more than they do now as a grown adult. Considering it was detrimental that I fit in back then. The awkward and confusing time that is puberty that I spoke on and the transition from not caring to be noticed, to wanting to attract attention. Before social media, the way we received this attention was far different than the times now. Expressing like or dislike is based on a notification rather than a glance or body language. Everyone's approval from others has been linked to the idea that the amount of people who positively react or interact with a post corresponds with your social acceptance. Not receiving enough likes, would lead to not feeling noticed and unimportant. Leaving the masses relying on the virtual world to determine their self-worth, when it's driven by your sole opinion and shouldn't be dictated by the number of hearts on a photo. The amount of power given over to others to approve or deny our life choices, looks, or status has controlled this new way of thinking. Easily accessible and able to achieve that acceptance by a mere post of a photo. How did our parents know people accepted them in the past? When they felt inadequate, where was their instant relief? Oh yeah…there wasn't any. There wasn't this amount of pressure given to other people to make their judgments as it wasn't at their fingertips. Instead, they had an image of their self-formed in their mind, and played off their view, rather than worrying about others. Now, I'm not saying insecurity escaped the generations before technology, I'm just saying it was easier to escape from and wasn't able to linger. How others view us has surpassed our own view on ourselves and has been able to dictate our overall self. My goal is to take that back! Starting with your self-confidence first, building that up to where you feel secure, and only allowing in a positive flow of opinions that have your best interest. Stepping away from the virtual world to improve the everyday, physical life that matters! You see these super edited photos of people online and then in person they are NOTHING like they post exposing their truest insecurities. Your phone can create an unrealistic version of you, exposed to everyone that isn't involved in your everyday, feeding this fake ego that isn't even the true you. Changing the way, you view yourself even being able to edit out what you thought was the bad, and still not feeling enough! wild.

Now, what if we cut off that source. What if you took away the ability to create this false persona and were able to be raw? Undeniably ourselves. Not worried if the picture was able to portray our best selves, but believed we were just that and walked with that confidence physically. Accepting our flaws, being content with who we were created to be, and didn't have to uphold any kind of status to appease others. Now of course we love attention, speaking for myself and want to attract attention, but how about the RIGHT attention. No more meaningless interactions or fueling the ability to allow others to morph us from their judgement. Being able to brush off what doesn't provide us guidance or the ability to allow us to grow. As opinions can be helpful, the continuous strive to be this perfect image that others have created is not. Wanting to be a better version of yourself is a fantastic goal, but not for the purpose of appeasing others or growing your follower count. Basically, what I'm trying to say is, focus on the opinions that matter. The ones who hold you close and care for your overall well-being and not what looks like there perfect moment captured. Allow others to see the confidence you hold within yourself, the security of who you are, and the unbothered reaction from their judgments.

These questions and concepts I found useful to help navigate how I saw my ideal self, beyond the laptop and phone. The person that I aspire to be all the time, out in the real world. The third and final psychological perception that we all may think about but not execute. How long has it been since you've stepped away fully from social media and focused on just you? Being disconnected from everyone's posts, posting, or sharing yourself, and basically disappearing on every platform to just live. Not focused on how you see yourself now, think you are viewed by other people, but the person you aspire to be. What are things that bring you pure joy, ease your mind, and or things you want to accomplish? Who is the person staring back at you in the mirror and are you truly happy with who he/she is, and how can you improve? I used to get lost in these questions as if they were so complicated to answer. Saying, I like certain things, or I'm happy with this and not that. Picking and choosing my favored characteristics. Not really stepping back and looking at me as a whole and what I can do to morph me into someone I loved and accepted fully. It felt like this unrealistic destination and impossible to accomplish, the ideal image of who I was proud of. How was I going to be happy with myself for ALL that I am? My life kind of felt like a series of events that I couldn't control that would morph me one way or another. The people I surrounded myself with dictated my mood as I was easily susceptible to their emotions, and it was draining. My financial situation wasn't always the best, so I had to lean on someone for support whether that be parents or a significant other to progress. I just felt like I couldn't stand on my two feet by myself, so how was I able to answer the question of who I was if I didn't know solely or how I was supposed to be my best self without help. Feeling lost and unable to pinpoint, I set out on a self-love, disconnected journey that involved myself and the ones I choose to be a part of the adventure trying to find the balance and growth. This expedition wasn't something that could have been solved with just one life changing trip or a strong week of completing healthy goals. It was an expansion of months compiled together of things that made ME happy and putting my best foot forward. I wanted to live a good/happy life to be the best me, so that's what I set out to do.

First thing I decided to do was get a vision. A clear picture of who I wanted to be and how I wanted to make others feel. I wanted to be someone that was a source of positive energy and could provide as much service to the ones I love while also being content with myself. The person you can always call if in a bind, or someone to always lend an ear without judgment. As I would want the same. I thought I was already decent at this skill but brining attention to it in the real world made me more self-aware of my reactions. Listening more than speaking and allowing others to find comfort in my presents. Reason being, I realize how my hard my life felt with more than enough negativity surrounding and not having someone to express it to left bottled up, unsolved on the inside created no solution to feel any better. If I was able to be open for others, I know they would do the same in return. Creating the effect of connectivity between people who genuinely care. Building my safe place and my clan of support that would be there in case I fell. Allowing others inside my mind made it easier to connect and feel accepted. There's no point in keeping negative or unresolved emotions to yourself as you'll feel like you're fighting a never-ending battle on your own. Improving the way, I interacted with others along with creating a smaller, stronger inner circle made my life feel more stable to kick start positive change. Not allowing others to intrude and plague it with unnecessary stressors. This best vision of myself was able to see the world for what it is and alter it for what I needed it to be. Being in the moment, focusing on my day to day of what I was given and embracing new opportunities that appeared.

This best vision of self is something I viewed as healthy and happy through whatever was thrown my way, not relying on others approval of success yet manifesting my own and attracting that same energy. Accomplishing goals, complete confidence, and security moving through life. No other rubric I had to follow, other than mine and what I deemed important to be the best version. Not that I was finishing first in everyone else's idea of life but finishing strong in what I created and found import- ant. While not having the social media outlets I was so accustomed too, I downloaded a self-affirmation app that would send me positive mantras to repeat up to ten times a day. In replace of others acceptance, I spoke into existence my own. Rewiring my brain to believe for itself. Proving that no other opinion in this transformation in my life was important but my own. Creating a life, my life into something positive rather than viewing it for what it wasn't. This was my journey to transform my life, as it might be useful to you, or maybe not at all. But one way or another, you must start somewhere.

Start by creating your own vision of who you want to be. Draw it out, create a plan, and then get started! No one has better intentions for yourself then you. Repeating positive habits can only lead you in those directions, agreeing with the opposite. If you continue to do what doesn't make you happy, you will be just that. You're able to shake up your life and uncap endless potential for who you invasion yourself to be. You just must start. Creating all positive answers to who you see yourself as now, how you think others view you, and the idea of your ideal self in the future all in real time. Not virtually.

CHAPTER 4:

SELF-ASSESSMENT

O f course we all tend to be on the indefinite search of who we are. Some get lost in the idea. But wonderfully, sciences have been able to evaluate our way of thinking allowing us to extort our mind in a way to receive these answers. The study of human assessments dates to the early days of the first World War. Seeing as they needed a heavy number of recruits in such a short amount of time. These administered tests sought out by professionals were able to not only measure the intelligence of someone, but also personality, brain function, and be able to decide the best suitable stationing for that soldier. Just as the way we take career placing tests now! As they did not have the time to invest into each candidate on a trial-and-error basis. This newly found concept was able to open the door to many educators to alter and be able to apply this technique in all areas including forensics, therapy, and as stated career. Searching for answers, humans were now able to evaluate our brain functions and provide many sought out questions including the daunting idea of who we are and how to improve oneself. The new study found as the therapeutic assessment by clinical psychologist Stephen Finn is defined as "a short-term intervention in which traditional psychological tests are used collaboratively with clients to help them understand themselves better and find solutions to their persistent problems"[6] for the result of therapeutic self-discovery.

Using both the mind of the clinical professional and the motivation of the assessed for one common goal of self-improvement. Being able to understand the information that has been observed by others, accumulated with the goal of self-awareness, and implementing a conclusion of just that. By explaining this information, by no means do I exert the need of a medical professional but having someone in-tune with self-improvement and providing guidance of where to start would be nothing but helpful. Seeing as they would be unbiased and able to see with a clear, educated mind where you might be able to add or tweak perception and reactions. Having a clear goal of your identity along with having the ability to develop your person, overcoming traumas, anxiety, or insecurities will lead you down a path of nothing but positive success and one step closer to achieving the happy life you sought out! The motivation you hold to improve your circumstance is where it starts and enduring the uncomfortable change on your own is key. Having a medical profession help guide you in the common goal of yourself improvement is just like a race car driver seeking a mechanics advice to help modify his/her car to perform better. As in my reading, many professionals doubted this method as it wasn't intensive enough. Seeing as the real change came from the assessed and just mostly minuscule guidance from the professional as time progressed. Seeing as it wasn't intensive enough for the more at risk of clients. But what if we take this concept and can evaluate our own self-assessment, as we have endless resources from the internet and are able to make a guide for our own self-improvement with the right amount of motivation? Cutting out the middleman. Not seeing our situation as "at risk" but more of knowing there is room for mental improvement and accepting the resources at bay. Being able to pinpoint our weakness' and altering the way we experience them moving forward. You have endless resources including extensive personality tests that can specifically pinpoint your personality, strengths and weakness', love, and relationships and how you react or need to be catered too. Through a lengthy questionnaire, created by professionals, we have the access to this information and can adjust from there! Personally, I've taken a quiz of this magnitude as directed from one of my old PH. D boss' I worked for, as he was trying to determine the best roll and suitable positions for all employees starting at a new location at his new office opening. (16personalitlies. com) Since taking the test, I've referenced it over a handful of times and even share it to new love interest, so they are allowed to get a grasp on my personality. It was scary accurate seeing as a computer could formulate my personality off how I answered questions. Resulting in a lengthy report of nothing but information on who I am and how my brain seems to be wired []. Now, since I had this information so accessible, how will I be able to use it for good I thought, other than just presenting it as a physical dating profile. Being able to break down my personality traits and assess ways others like me think, gave myself a whole other perspective seeing a layout of who I was summed up in one report. Take the test I've referenced above and evaluate your outcome. Let's get an idea of who we are. You'll be impressed on how well this system is able to define you. Make sure to be honest and think the questions through, thoroughly answering to the best of your ability. You're basically getting a free, at home assessment minus the office appointment and copay!

It's comforting knowing a little more about yourself and feeling secure in the person you perceive to be. Taking the quiz gave me a new confidence in who I was, knowing the way I am and how to interact better with the world I surround myself with. Now moving forward, determining if the self-questioning aspects you are experiencing are modifiable or non – modifiable is the hard part. As the test concluded, it might have had you face some hard truths while also giving you an idea clear idea of how to alter what's currently giving you a hard time. Self-worth? Relationships? Career? Are these conscious choices you are making yourself that are allowing this downfall your experiencing? Allowing and implementing actions unknowingly that are going against your personality that allows low self-esteem and demised self-worth to creep in and find a home in your brain. Are you able to shake the constant need of reassurance of other judgments and stand on what are just your two feet? Whatever the self-doubting aspects maybe, pinpointing what is the cause is the only way to correct the imperfection in your mind and knowingly change if it's your doing, or others. Clearly, there are always traits we can improve but acknowledging the change and self-perseverance that needs to happen is the place to kick start that change you seek. Think to yourself, what is crucial to change for myself improvement? Beyond what I'm doing currently, or what others have insisted. Sit with yourself and embrace where your anxieties take you and take innovatory if you can conquer them through your own empowered will. Determining our own variables and configuring our own characteristic to sort out a different outcome of our lives than the one currently presented. I don't think that sounds too hard considering you're just evaluating yourself and you're the best for the job! Especially if you have taken my advice to endure the online personality quiz, you've already had a fresh set of eyes on who you are! Asses what no longer serves you and write it down. Whether it may be a relationship with someone who you always seem to clash with, a new job you can't seem to find balance in, or constant self-doubt. Finding what's causing the turbulence and finding a solution to not give it precedence in your life anymore through your empowered motivation for a new positive life!

With my focus on social media and the mental toll it has taken on my generation and future, start by envision your life without it. Could this honestly be infecting your brain and not allowing you to see your life for what it is? Causing any mental trauma, anxieties, or harsh judgment you wish it wasn't? Self-inflicted or by others. Decide for yourself through your own experiences if it leans more positive or negative for your well-being. Decide which of the apps you feel more comfortable with and take note of the ones you could live without. They were created solely for our entertainment and clearly previous generations have gotten by just fine without. Consider if that would be a positive change to make for yourself and what possible impacts it could have on your future. Would you be missing out? Or would it allow you to narrow your life down to the people who affect it directly? Even if this feels like a small change to make...it will have a great affect by known experience. I don't think we realized how big of a toll social media has taken on our day-to-day yearning for that constant gratification and connection. Would you feel less important or seen? Or more comfortable in the physical life you are building for yourself? Either way, allow yourself to assess how much social media has conformed your day to day and be able to adjust accordingly!

One experience I have had since distancing myself from socials has been, I'm genuinely surprised when people tell me updates about friends, family, and accomplishments! I respond in exclamations and excitement rather than the constant, "Yeah. I saw you post about that.". Genuine, natural reactions in person rather than a secondary reaction created by the already widely shared news. The emotions that you can experience while in the moment of shared conversion, I've noticed, allows a deeper connection between you and that other person. Making the moment personal, rather for all to experience. Not knowing this was something I was missing out on and that my specific personality yearns for. Before stepping away from the virtual world, I never contracted this as a variable that I would want to focus on, yet I see it now as I've already changed my circumstance. Being able to reassess my new outcome and focus for my personal growth. Noticing, it's not just myself who will benefit, but others who are surrounded. Myself noticing that social media was huge cause for my mental downfall, taking the initiative to remove and revaluate causing a chain reaction of positivity for how I live out my new every day. Not worried about the notifications that pop up on a screen rather than how others are feeling while in my presence. My mind has been able to alter itself back to what I've called factory settings, as I was never worried about my virtual self or staying "connected" when growing up. It's something that has changed our society as a whole and becoming disconnected allows our mind to focus on the simpler aspects of life as to what we find most important. Reassessing who I am, considering what I've brought to light in my personality assessment, minus all the noise that usually was able to cluster my mind. Seeing as being more present in my day to day rather than with my eyes stuck to a screen, has fueled the interpersonal connection I sought out with the ones closest to me. Starting and ending everyday with just myself subtracting others input and applying new strategies of connection. Noticing through the assessment, now brining light to my personality on paper, where I can start to feel more sufficient in the areas that weren't as dominant. Seeing as the test collaborates your mind, energy, nature, tactics, and identity allowing myself to understand what makes me tick. Pointing arrows at the reasons certain areas have been unsuccessful considering it was clashing with my personality or simply I've been forcing an outcome that had no business being a part of my journey. Reasons why past relationships haven't been successful or the job I'm currently in hasn't provided any positive sustenance. Creating this newly defined life of all that serves me a positive purpose rather than fighting against the current and expecting a greater outcome. Embracing who we are after defining who that is and moving forward with a new, fully indulged view on the part you play as well as others.

CHAPTER 5:

WHAT WE VALUE

L et's dig a little deeper. Rather than focusing on what appears on the surface, what are the core principles that you choose to follow? The guidelines you use to dictate your life by defining the structure to what you hold important. Whether you are aware of your personal values or not, everyone has them and are what defines the building blocks of the decisions you make in all areas of the life you are choosing. These values are what dictate your decision making and becoming more aware of what they are can help you live a more specifically designed, happier life for yourself. As they do differ from person to person, if I haven't made that point crystal clear yet, that everyone is so incredibly different, these values determine what you invest your time, money, and over all attention too and where they rank on your importance list. Without knowing, we already display what we value to others even if you aren't consciously making the decisions. An accumulation of these decisions is what define your destined reality of what you choose to build your life off. Whether it be strong family importance, a successful career, or religion, these examples are forces that you choose to define your time spent on earth. They could be positive or negative and what you choose to invest your time into will ultimately determine the course their life. As a child, your parents instill these core values and try to navigate you through what they believe is right and wrong until you can alter those decisions for yourself. In the mild chance you come from a broken home, didn't have strong parental figures, or some other form of a rough upbringing, these values could have been skewed in all sorts of ways left for you to navigate on your own. Starting the whirl wind that is an altered reality you weren't prepared for, unless taught different. Prime example: if a young boy growing up witness' his father disrespecting his mother, he will more than likely tend to do the same to his spouse, unconsciously considering it was never a value the man in the house he saw as his life educator held value too. Until he is taught different. Your core values tend to change as your life alters into adulthood. Repositioning the focus you have, trying to define how to create the life you want. Controlling the type of people, you surround yourself with, the amount of focus you put on certain aspects, and the quality of things you allow to flow in and out. Negative core values only lead to a negative life. Just like my pervious concepts I've spoken on thus far. If you put an unhealthy amount of focus on aspect that won't benefit you, or values that will help you achieve your goals, then you will just be a hamster on a wheel. Stuck in the same place, confused, and frustrated. Without understanding what you hold value too, there will be a very low possibility you are living the life you are seeking. Being unsure is a great place to start, seeing as it can be a blank canvas for you to design. You can visualize the person you hope to grow into and transform your life accordingly. You are a product of your environment, so why not create that environment into what you want it to be.

Write them down. Just like large companies and their mission statements. Get a base of where you see your life and all that you wish to surround it with. Maybe what you've been focused on in the pass is no lover serving you in this new season of your life and it's time to recalibrate. Or you wish to see yourself in a different light, living a different way that you feel more content with. Good news, it's all controllable and in the palm of your hands. This past year, I put a huge effort into my religion and becoming stronger in my faith as I didn't before. It was a value that I was taught at a young age, but never really invested energy into. Yes, I would pray every other night and for the ones who needed strength occasionally, but I wanted to feel secure in what I forever kept on the back burner of a half-assed following. Now, I'm just using this as an example, so please stick with me even if our beliefs are different. The concept just applies and hopefully by experience gives me structure to speak from. After my breakup I spoke on earlier, I felt lost. The constant control I endured left me empty and confused as to who I was. I sought out the wrong attention on social media, looking for my outlet. Leaving me just as empty as I started. I had to construct a new person and who I was going to grow into on my own. So, I had to restructure. I wrote a list of goals and things that I would pour my time into until accomplished to hopefully build me a new, better me. Confident and whole heartily the person I choose. Along with getting back into shape by running miles a day which I swore I would never do, rebuilding my relationships with close ones, and my faith were all at the top of the list.

I always was a believer, but growing up with the father I did, it was hard to put full trust in a church who turned a blind eye. We would be there every Sunday, attended vacation bible school every summer, and our extended families even were a part of every sermon and offering weekly. Yet, when my father would show up and boast about how great him and our family dynamic was, it all felt like a joke. So, I revolted. I used to draw on all the prayer cards in the pews; butterflies, fake nails on the praying hands, and put them back in their place like I never did anything of the sort. Refusing to dress up leaving my Sunday best to be a hoodie and yoga pants presenting, I did in fact just roll out of bed and I did not want to be there. Not stepping into another church beyond funerals and weddings as I blossomed into my adult years. I still, what I call "believed" but like I said, it really was just routine. Until I decided to make it one of my core's values, I wanted to build the new me off. I choose that this was something I wanted to be a part of who I was and my every day. I wanted everyone to know how confident I was in my life, providing me with the security I so desperately searched for. I wanted to get rid of this anxiety I so heavily experienced daily, the doubting of myself worth, and through my faith I knew it would be possible. So, I tried. But in my own way. No structure if I was going forward with what I believed correctly, or a rubric to follow. I just did what brought me peace and made the more than conscious decision to invest myself into what I was indulging in. Listening to sermons on my commute to work, followed by repetitive prayers when I would overcome with wounding anxiety. Daily versus and quick studies to hopefully start my day off positive. I just continued to invest myself, for myself, by myself. As time passed, six months in I noticed small changes. Nothing major. Allowing myself to accept that this process was a jog, not a sprint just like my newly found workout routine. Then, one day I received gratification. My stepfather, who I respect to no end, and I were having a conversation of a life triggering event of me losing my job. Stressed as it was out of my control, worried how I would pay my bills, he simply replied, "what do you always tell everyone else to do?". Halted by the question, I looked deep into my brain to search for one of the sarcastic quotes I usually stapled my life by. Finding no answer, he replied, "pray on it and leave it to God" …. I say that. Me? And enough times for it to be something others associate me with? Instant gratification flooded my veins as I knew I was transforming! I made it apparent to myself that my religion will be a part of me, yet now others are seeing it as well. It was simple acts daily that did not take up much time, but because I decided that this is what I held true value too, my faith, that it allowed me to morph myself into someone who has just that! Not doing it with any other agenda than myself and creating a better future for who I planned to be. Trusting the process and relying on myself, knowing I had the best intentions. Being able to relearn and create my own definition of my newfound value and carrying it with me, knowing its importance.

Choosing to redefine my values was a choice I made because I knew I was better than where I was. Reflecting on who I use to be, I needed to take action to change my circumstance and how I viewed my life. After having my list of what I wanted to accomplish, starting, and making it a habit was the only struggle. I found what worked for me even taking breaks from what I made routine and allowing myself to reassess. This was a process, and I wasn't sure if it was something that would stick or not. I didn't want to feel like I was trying to force the comfort I ever so searched for in my newfound faith. It needed to be natural and easy. Creating these new life values were something I had to 100% believe in. They couldn't be something imaginary that went against who I'm programed to be. If you choose new core values off what sounds good, you will forever be clashing with an uncomfortable transition. As these are the basis of your life, specifically chosen by you, so wouldn't you want them catered to your needs? Whether its other aspects such as honesty, respect, or creativity (etc.) … there's so many types to choose from that redirects your mission in life. Below I included a table of examples… Circle two you wish to focus on or create your own if you think of something different! They can be ones from your list before, or that you are already aware of or something new you wish to conspire. Then let's discuss how to bring more attention to these new core values you've brought to light and only allowing positivity to manifest through!

Dependability	Consistency	Motivation	Courage
Reliability	Honesty	Positivity	Education
Loyalty	Efficiency	Optimism	Service to Others
Commitment	Faith	Respect	Patriotism
Open-Mindedness	Compassion	Fitness	Relationships

You've picked your two, correct? Now, let's combine all the core values of the person you are today, plus the ones you would like to make a part of the transformed you of the future. This doesn't need to be lengthy process. More of an eye opener. Many of us haven't taken the time to draw and outline of our life and recognize the main structures that dictate it.

But you've already invested your energy into this book, hopefully looking for answers and here we are. Today is your day! Compile your list and take mental inventory all that you've circled or written down. Now, we need to rank in importance. However, many values you've accumulated, what's number one? And follow down the list of what you want the source that drives your life to stem from. See as there is no negativity as there is no more room for that on your journey. Take a moment to rest and evaluate how you can apply these values every day and uphold their importance. Whether it's spending more time with your family, exerting more effort into your career, or simply being able to focus on the positive, these small acknowledgments and efforts can go a long way! Sometimes even creating a vision board will help remind you. Being able to capture your attention and bring more self-awareness of the core values you've now or will continue to live your life by.

So, as we're on this journey of our new self-discovery and can unlock the consciousness that are our core values, we notice that this has already been just a journey taken solo. We are exploring our true selves and creating this life we can be content with beyond any other outside opinions. Learning what basis our lives are built off and applying it to our future. Whether you have deleted social media or not as I highly suggested, or just stepping away for a few months, being able to apply all these values in every aspect is detrimental to your metamorphosis you seek. Yes, starting physically, but if you decide to keep your virtual self, it's important to uphold these standards you have set for yourself going forward through all forms. If you decided to keep your socials or just one or two, purge what no longer serves you. Do you still follow your ex that loves to post things out of spite? Do you get anxiety via the amount of likes you get or don't get on a picture? Whatever you feel no longer should be a part of this process should now be abolished. To possibly be returned when you have a new mindset or when you maybe decide it no longer has a space for your newfound path. Whatever is a cause for an interruption of self-growth and leads to comparison or self-doubt should not be a part of your everyday. Especially when you don't have the positive mental capacity to endure it. Social media has now made a huge dent into our everyday and some jobs even depend on it. Whether it be marking our communication. Sometimes it's not as easy as deactivating an account which I understand. But why continue to view different posts that cause negative emotions or keep the open flow of other judgments at the tips of your fingers? There's just no reason for it. As I stated, I decided to keep my snapchat. I deactivated my forever daily revolving door of what was Facebook (mainly for friends and family), Instagram (flaunting my life to ex's and want to be ex's lol) and Twitter (whoever else). I felt as if I had so many memories saved on my snap app, and I loved being able to accumulate videos and pictures of places I've been and to include others who are close to me. Adding certain filters, or geo tags, it was a way for me to store memories beyond just my camera roll, yet I was not opening my ventures to the whole world, just all who I accept. I deleted followers as they no longer served a purpose in my life, which honestly, I might have done too often. As I would date, and they would fail, I would always remove them as the anxiety of them moving on was not something I wanted to endure. As friendships passed and no lover served me…. delete. I would remove people that made me feel like I was posting for them. For them to see I was cool or to notice me in any way. The second I knew I was posting for someone else, gone. As time rolled on, I noticed my viewers became fewer and fewer and I only kept people who profited positive sustenance to the things I decided to share. Workout snaps, vacations, or simply funny moments, I only opened my life up to others who were able to enjoy rather than judge. As I no longer caught attention and approval, the app became less meaningful and more as a convenience to send media. I was already conversing with these people outside the app, no longer yearned for attention, and wasn't worried who noticed what I posted because I specifically approved of each one that had access. Being able to build off genuine connection from the real world and applying our interactions over an app only made our bond stronger as they weren't accumulations of meaningless, attention seeking cries for help. Not saying that's how all snap chatters used the app, but I would get puzzled responses as to why I never snapped more often, or why my snap score is so low. Well…. because I'm out living and focusing on the relationships that matter. My attention had been given so easily where it didn't feel like I was seen yet more as lost in a jumble of notifications on other people's phones. I wanted to be more than that. Limiting my time on the social app, along with deleting who no longer served my physical life, narrowed down the intentions of the ones who sat back and made their comments. It looks away the heaviness of the posts. No longer worried about back lash or the weirdness of "is this socially acceptable to put on my story?". We've all been there. Yet, being able to free your mind of the underlying judgmental chains that dictated what you were able to share or not was liberating! I could post the same selfies or the same "type" of selfie two days or even two hours in a row and not care because why? Because everyone who viewed it knew that I was just me doing me, or they knew what I was doing that day and could have a little detail inside my journey. Either way, the constant anxiety of posting diminished over time since it turned into me posting for me and not for me to be seen. I wasn't trying to impress, but more as show off for myself.

Social media was formed to keep people connected, as well as them being able to share experiences of personal growth with the ones they hold close, or even knew people they meet. Allowing others, a peek into your life and providing support or comfort in whatever we decided to share. I mean, that's why "like" buttons were created. Yet somewhere down the road, they became competitions of appearance and status. Showing others how much better you're off compared to where they are. Boasting about life changes and momentous achievements conquered. Leaving out the trials fought through and the days of gray. If we now can recalibrate their meanings to fit our lives now and make them beneficial and full of positivity or realness, what would that mean and look like? Considering we are the first generation to grow up using this new technology and only followed the rules and regulations given. Are we able to redefine how social media is used and how we respond? Instead of the number of friends added as an achievement, how about knowing all your followers personally? How weird does that sound? I know for a fact on my old Instagram account I had over six hundred followers, but I think I invited about ten people to my birthday party. What if clearing out the accumulation of attention seekers and being able to provide life progression content to others who were a part of your journey was the destination? What if the content we saw was of greater value rather than for quick satisfaction? If you choose to keep your socials, discover a new way of using them that can benefit your newfound values rather than for meaningless amusement. What if social could be used as a tool instead? Sift through follows and following. Only allow those you know or have had a connection with. Limit the number of eyes on your active sharing, if you choose to stay virtual. Honestly, if they don't have the effort to physically see, talk, or be near you, chances are they no longer serve you any propose. Value your time and the ones you allow to accumulate it. Be able to apply those newly found core values and show you who sits behind the screen rather than entertaining a false ego to show off to others who don't matter. Dispose of all you follow that make you feel less than. Only accepting attention from others who have the same goals as you, surrounding your inner circle of nothing but positive support and discovering the weak links in your life to apply more attention to. You're able to do these changes all through your own motivated will and you're the one making the rules! If you care enough to listen to your little inner voice of where it pulls you, being able to manifest it should be nothing but tweaking what you're already doing!

CHAPTER 5:

ROLE MODELS

Remember being asked as a child over and over the question of, "what do you want to be when you grow up?". Adults looking to you for an imaginative or overly optimistic answer of a Unicorn Flyer or a Veterinarian. Something that was able to display your personality and or goals you wish to achieve on the road to adulthood. Parents priding themselves off the answer of their children. I recall in my elementary school class we had a project of the sort. We took home a poster drawing outlining a human and we were supposed to draw/design the person we saw our future self as and come dressed exactly alike the following day. Parents were involved as it was included as a small career day for my first-grade class. Being so excited I knew exactly what I wanted to be! My mom.

Bringing home, the project, excited to draw myself as the woman who was helping me, I couldn't be prouder to show the rest of my class. Yet, my mother's job was nothing close to glamourous. She was an employee at our counties water department in charge of billing and accounts, which she had been for years. She questioned my decision as if I wasn't sure this is what I wanted to present. As if other kids knew about water bills and what happened for delinquent accounts. My drawing project started off with a normal pair of pants, casual shirt, and the coolest name badge that had a retractable string that didn't involve unclipping it from your person.

Which I thought was beyond neat and my mother yelling at me from fiddling with it all the time, as if I were going to break it. I wanted one myself and had the chance. The drawing was just, normal. No brief case or fancy doctor's jacket. No magic or made-up dream job. Just me, following in my favorite persons footsteps. The morning of the project, my mother laid out my black dress pants and my fanciest top which, I believe was just a colored V-neck and I was ready to go. Looking nothing but office casual. We headed off to my school, ready to present who I saw as my future self and couldn't be more eager.

Entering the classroom, all the parents stood in the back as each child, one by one would present. My turn arrived as I explained the importance of the Lake County Utilities, gleaming my bright smile at my mother knowing I was making her proud along with every other boring office employee. Yet, she knew my presentation wasn't about the career. I hung the drawing of myself in the hallway next to the police officers and surgeons proud as people asked questions of why I choose what I did. I remember my favorite line being "if you're mean to me, my mom can shut your water off" using it as leverage and ammo toward others I felt inadequate compared to. That quickly faded as everyone became older and wiser to unlawful utility mismanagement and no longer induced fear in my bullies. But it was a power I saw my mother have and to me, she was the almighty. Looking back, I couldn't imagine my daughter not wanting to explore the unlimited range of possible carriers and settling on one I choose out of pure convenience. I'm aware the job my mother had fallen into wasn't her first choice nor her dream job. In fact, I remember her complaining a lot about mistreatment and lack of recognition, yet that still is what I wanted to display to pursue. She made it seem more elaborate creating this wonderland of adulthood that I one day would enter. Bring your child to work day, consisted of a small desk behind her cubicle eating at McDonald's and minuscule filing. All her coworkers knew of us (her children as I have two older brothers and one younger sister) and we were the little ducklings to our mother hen. An unfamiliar group of women who watched us grow and all greeted us with smiles and open candy dishes as we would visit the office once every few months transforming into a second family over the years. She didn't make much, as if knew, yet she did the most and what should for her rambunctious offspring. She never once faltered or showed weakness, yet now as an adult hearing she had twenty dollars to live off for two weeks or an hourly wage slightly above minimum was astonishing. Not airing out her dirty laundry, but this woman was able to create a secure home, and more than elaborate childhood filled with adventure and all I wanted without us being aware of her struggles. She was and forever will be my role model, which is the message I knew I wanted to portray even in the early days of elementary school. Of course, my classmates had no idea why I choose that career, or what it even was. Our little brains couldn't grasp the concept I was trying to convey behind the career, a heroic mother who I saw as everything I wanted to be.

I was more than blessed, excluding my abusive father to have such a strong parental figure guiding me as I navigated my adolescent years. Honestly, I have no idea how I would have turned out if it wasn't for her strength, patience, and constant behavioral correction. Because of the mistreatment I endured from my father, I was very internally angry. For years, leading me on this expedition to be happy within myself for who I am and eager for who I am becoming as an adult. Taking control of my own destiny, forever on the endless search to surround myself with things that serve me a positive purpose, never to return to the negative, angry days. Yes, as my father was absent, the time we did spend with him was full of mental/emotional abuse and narcissistic drunken behavior, as I wasn't able to control my surroundings leaving my brothers and I to experience a life we never would have chosen. This chapter, I want to dive into my background as not many people get the chance to express their story leading to the person they are now and hopefully connect with ones who need to understand they are not a product of their upbringing and more of the conscious choices they accumulate now.

My two older brothers and I were in an ongoing custody battle between my mother and my father until I, the youngest out of the three, turned 16 years old and was the legal age to make our own conscious decision of where we wanted to stay. Before then, we would transfer between the two houses, a week with mom and then a week with dad. Packing a bag of belongings to shuffle between the two houses. The structure in each couldn't be more different. My father, being intoxicated for most of the time would treat us as if we were in bootcamp, as constant yard work and house chores had to be done. Compared to my mother who only had us tidy our rooms and my new baby sister awaiting eagerly for "her kids" as she called us, to come back from our unshared father's house. We were on or own most days to explore, play, and come up with our own daily routine on our fathers' weeks as he was off trying to find a new stepmom. Women would come and go. I would spend time with this new lady and that new lady, and by the end of the week a different would be at the house. Until one week retuning to our fathers, a new woman who we have never encountered and her three kids, from three different fathers may I add, were fully moved into what was our childhood home, entering my new reality of sharing my room with a stranger. All of us shoved together, not familiar with one another compiling a household of eight bodies to form a more than dysfunctional family. This new woman, as I would eventually call stepmom, was roughly TWENTY-TWO years younger than my father. Him exceeding the age of her own dad, just to add even more perspective. The most unstable couple, now responsible for six little influential minds to from for half the time, as we all had different parents awaiting outside that house. With this new family dynamic, tempers would flair, manipulations would increase, and abuse arose as she was nothing but an addition to my fathers messed up antics. Leaving all of us scarred with some type of mental or emotional trauma to overcome as we were able to escape the detriments of their bad parenting.

Years passed as our minds continued to be scrambled by the change in structure and unpredictability. My mom uses to say she had to "reverse the brain washing" every other week to get her kids back. The kids she knew and so aggressively tried to raise in a correct manor minus the chaos. As we would act one way on her weeks, sweet, caring, and compassionate compared to the tempered, manipulative, and aggressive nature we expressed at our fathers. As it was instinctual and what we accumulated to survive in that environment. Unknowing of the actual damage that my father and new stepmother were doing, until I became an adult and the trauma still followed. Turning away from my mother as my protector seeing her as an enemy, not knowledgeable of all she had done to keep me from the pain and the malicious acts on the other side of my family. Her constant structure became too much as I felt constantly pulled in different directions. Growing into my teenage years, finally able to form my own options and actions, rebellion fallowed. Her unknowingly pushing me away. Turning to different forms of role models I wanted to design my life alike, I was on the hunt. The media provided an easy outlet. The perfect image of an independent successful woman was my new destination. Rebranding my view of something out of reach, rather than in my means trying to escape what I've known for so long. I didn't want nor to need anyone, I thought to myself. It was my time to create my own path. Seeing as adults who are independent and self-sufficient can control their environments, I had to hurry the process up to get to where I needed to be. Pushing her away and revolting her parenting, only to loop back around once the real world chewed me up and spit me back out. I knew from a young age that my mom was everything I wanted to embody. Why someone else was able to alter my vision or the fact that I gave them the ability or power to do so was a learning lesson. But somehow, the values instilled in me, were deeply rooted. Her letting me go to figure out the world, as I felt like I needed to at the young age of nineteen, only to return a short year later. Learning I took a short detour and needed that guidance. Her guidance as it has not failed me. I choose her as a role model from the very moment I acquired consciousness and continue to follow her stride as much as I can through my adult years. We have the same values, as I tend to be more adventurous, risky, and outspoken. She is someone I know that can lead me toward the success that I seek. Not only because she has proved herself time and time again of being an incredible mother that I aspire to be, but her work ethic, ability to provide, and the way she carries herself all embodies the person I see as hopefully myself one day. As I could choose anyone else, possibly a movie star, an author perhaps, or any other family member. But luckily enough, I didn't have to travel far to find my inspiration and as much as I pushed away, the universe always corrected my direction as my values carried me back to the person I trusted. My role models.

As we mature, we decide who we want to be. Who we surround ourselves with, where we work, and overall, the amount of effort we put into being what our definition of successful? It can be successful in your career, relationships, or individually. It's all based off your own values as we have narrowed down. Yet the journey taken to get to your goals and who you choose to include is detrimental to your growth. Who are the people you look up to? Any celebrities in mainstream media? Family members like I have. Whose posts are you flooding your feed with and giving your attention to? The reality of these questions determines over all how you see yourself and whether these role models are realistic or not and can provide you with either a positive or negative connotation of yourself image. Let's say my role model is any of the Kardashians. Whether it be adolescent me, or adult me, the image that they portray is nothing but the dollar sign and plastic surgery. My opinion....and making money off the average mass of females that aspire to be their definition of beautiful and wealthy. As they are some of the most sought out females of this era. Even though all we see of them is surface, as they are master manipulators of the media and can only show what they want. Do we know their true values? Know them personally? Or only what they post or show on tv, editing out the bad and changing their face when a slight imperfection is brought to light. Having someone in the media is not a healthy role model as you don't KNOW them. There's no way by keeping up with their media feeds you're able to know the person behind the screen even though you might feel that misconstrued connection. Setting realistic expectations for yourself and including the same in others who you follow will lead you toward a path of higher success rather than disappointment from unrealism. Determining who is detrimental for your season of growth and who will mutually benefit from your follow, not only showing the prefect image but the raw imperfections that floods everyone's life. Choosing my mother was something I consciously made the decision of as a child, that was lost in my teens and regained in my adulthood. As I did have celebrities, I gawked over which led me stray and empty as life stressors continued to happen for me, yet somehow not to them? It clicked that what I was inspiring to be wasn't a realistic goal yet only an image the actor themselves were perfectly portraying. Making money off my attention. It never brought me full comfort or direction, seeing as they didn't know me, nor knew of my situation, yet still acted as if they did. You know what really made my head spin. The constant bikini pictures from the Instagram models. You know, when they started posting the "IG vs Reality" captioned pictures. Exposing the immaculate ability to position their body and wear certain clothing that successfully hid imperfections in a captured moment. Younger me thinking, "ugh I wish I looked like that". Yet, it was all perception. Now, I had a strong capable woman related to me, right in front of me who embodied inside and out all that I wanted to be. That has been through true hell and back, beautiful as ever (I mean for real you should see my mom) and someone who always had my best interest at heart. Comparing to the online perfectly positioned, perfect skinned, distant human who only was a fake image. As I circled back to my mom, knowing this is who the real idea of guidance comes from and has given me the ability to alter myself accordingly. Altering meaning, taking what she has learned into consideration and applying it to my own experiences and beliefs. As I have my own idea for my life, the basic structure I wanted to build it off correlated to the same woman who brought me into this world and has given me a positive rubric to circle my life around.

As I had a strong leader that I specifically choose, I have been able to make over my inner self to be one that I can see as being just that for someone else one day. Growing up in the strange and altered circumstances I did, learning ways to cope and channel that mistreatment into something useful was a forever struggle until one day, it just wasn't. As I kept pushing for a better version on myself, forever altering my surroundings while sticking to my same values. Searching out others who had the same. I had the rubric my mother instilled and choose to listen too, now applying it to my life and even exceeding my own expectations was the goal. Defining my own path while creating this safe circle of people who surround me of the same internal goals. Choose wisely with whom you look up to. Whether it be someone in the media, make sure they are showing all sides of themselves and can express the struggles of everyday rather than hiding it away. Make sure your values align. It's easier to feel close to someone who shares the same structure you build your life off. A lot of the times we attract friends of the same values creating a stronger bond and connection as we tend to outgrow some friendships. Noticing when they no longer serve you or align with your destination. Surrounding yourself with only things that serve the same purpose you are seeking. Reassess who you are currently surrounding yourself with and the people you give most of your time too. How do they make you feel and how do you see them playing apart in the journey you are currently on? Are they advocates for your change and self-betterment, or the opposite? You've accumulated your values and now transforming who you allow to obtain your energy, hopefully adding to the process. Concluding everyday with being someone you are proud to be, so that your able to one day be a guide for others. Passing on the knowledge of self-discovery and positive transformation. Be a vessel for your friends and family allowing yourself to confidently carry out your core values and mutually benefit each other off the same beliefs. One day, confidently becoming your own role model and then someone else's.

CHAPTER 6:

ACCEPTING DISCOMFORT

Kick starting new habits and or pushing the boundaries of your comfortability welcomes the influence of inner change. As stated by an American professor, Ph. D, and LMSW who has dictated her life work to vulnerability courage states, "[...] we need to cultivate the courage to be uncomfortable and to teach the people around us how to accept discomfort as a part of growth." -Brené Brown [7], seeing it as a tool for self-betterment. Not viewing it as a something to falter from, but as a steppingstone. To be uncomfortable opens a door for change and possibility that your comfortableness wouldn't necessarily allow as you continually stick to the same old. Change and altered perspective in your environment from such courage, exposing the possibility of modification in all that surrounds your life currently. New friends, job opportunities, and or a newfound confidence. Whatever the comfortability keeping you stagnant is, masking the deeper anxiety for change. The ability to change your situation through actions and pushing your own boundaries is a tool many take for granted and shy away from, as its anything but fun. Deciding to finally do the one thing that's been scaring you or the opportunity that you've been drawing back from could potentially open the gate way that exerts you into the next phase of your life. Finding confidence through the unknown of your anxieties and not hesitating from the possible outcomes, standing strong to overcome whatever has been holding you back! Whether good or bad. As humans, we tend to stick to what we know. What's comfortable. We create routines, we stick to the same friend group, never exploring beyond our wildest boundaries so we can configure the destined outcome. Knowing we will be okay and are safe in our so far selected choices knowing already where the journey lead. Finding stability in what has already happened and shying away from change. Going out of that specific zone isn't something that most people enjoy, I mean why would they? Enduring the possible sweat attacks, nervous shakes, or stuttering that accompanies the fear. Yet, what could be the possibilities that wait along the line of your personally drawn boarder of comfortability? If instead of being afraid of the wrong choice or the repercussions, envision the idea of being able to find growth and new pathways in the newly gained knowledge from the experience. Taking the jump unknowing of the consequences, just acting on instinct. Accepting the idea that you may fail; you may be making the wrong choice but knowing your soul would transform from the initial decision, initiating inner change that was gained due to the vulnerable courage induced by the idea. Stepping into the world of discomfort, upsetting your everyday, forming new and sought-after perspective for the singular goal of inner change.

This perfect image I so harshly express is something we all wish to achieve, but sadly it's not realistic. As not one person who walks and breathes on this beautiful planet has conquered, even as so convincingly as others perceive they do. As we try to control our surrounding environments, we must understand and educated our minds to the idea that our trials and errors are what allow us to find what keeps us processing through our circumstance. Considering nothing ever stays the same. To not succeed is to correct the path taken to find something better, altering your reality pushing you into the next season, whatever that maybe for you. Forever changing and forever growing, deciding the direction of our future through our decisions and the followed outcome, good or bad. Understanding we are not where we were, or where we want to be, and accepting the bumpy path it might take to achieve that future destination we seek. Allowing the negative emotions to have just as much as an impact as the positive, opening the door for betterment no matter the conclusion. Focusing on the perspective we hold and controlling the areas we can yet being able to let go of what we cannot. Considering downfalls are a way of life and the construction of how you learn or bounce back determines the victory. Allowing the negative emotions, a space instead of shielding from the possible hardship trying to avoid these emotions, acting as if they aren't real. Failure should be seen as a building block to lead toward your life of success, accepting it as something to learn from. In this virtual world we have created that we allow to consume so much of our attention, it has only been able to display the unusually good and allow the insecurities to creep into our minds often when the outside world doesn't follow. Meaning have controlled so much of what we post that anything that might display a weakness or slight downfall of some sort will show you as unsuccessful compared to the masses. Displaying the image in your mind of never being enough. Successful enough, pretty enough. Whatever our insecurities have settled on and the online world being able to enhance those thoughts through comparison and controlled information shared. This person just bought a house while I still live at home. This person just got married and I'm still single. As beneficial as social media has been to keep people con-nected, it has also been given a platform of unlimited comparison of life events that has made us seem inadequate to our neighbors. When it's their season of nourishment and blessings, we tend to sigh as if we wished it was us. Even though the person posting had a positive connotation behind the sharing, the negative fallout that creeps into our own thoughts is that forever secured self-doubt. We feel as if there's always someone ahead of our laid-out path… even though our journeys are not even close to com-parable. Creating this never-ending doubt, food for your inner most anxi-eties keeping them alive rather than working towards killing them off. The creation of this controlled online environment has over time, created its own rubric, per app of what you should post to appear successful. When your life doesn't amount to the expectations for reasons that are beyond your control giving you no content to share, the need to achieve the false self-will over come to show off that yearned after success. Leading you down a dark road of lifelong expectations to uphold, while your day to day hasn't changed. Wanting to keep up with the others who are expressing their only positive experiences, but at the same time being crippled by the idea of not amounting to what others are accomplishing. As your journey isn't amounting to theirs. Eager to show off as well, the false self emerges and finds a way to fill the void temporarily. Entering the constant cycle of demised self-worth from the real world not amounting to what is being displayed and a constant chase to fill those empty voids for attention and achievement; like trying to fill up a bucket, full or water when it has a hole in the bottom. It will never work nor reach the top. Leading to you displaying one image, compared to how you feel and who you truly are in real life. A temporary fix for a deeply rooted feeling. What if we were able to discard those rubrics? Eliminating the expectations of what society has formed these apps to be and taking away their power of inadequacy. Accepting life's flaws which are more common than the distorted, allowing others to just focus on their path rather than the perfect image based on perspective. Revealing the power of authenticity displaying normalcy of the good and bad of life. Instead of impatiently waiting for the next blessing to post, embracing the season your currently in taking away life lessons for betterment even if it's not the greatest. Noticing your journey is not comparable to others and what is displayed just online is never the whole truth.

If setbacks are frowned upon in society, yet every human experiences them, why aren't we celebrating the victory over triumph? Everyday struggles and mental downfalls seem lonelier and harsher as people only want to brag about their success. Not giving the recognition to that hard path taken for them to finally achieve their success they sought out, or the determination of vulnerability it took to push through. How do we normalize the negatives we all experience? How do we alter the perception of the so called "failures" of life and modify them into something sought after as needed for growth? Now taking those extra judgments and voices away, the online audience, and subtracting the false self-projected of only positive experiences, where does just your opinion of yourself lead you and where is it you want to go? Personally, your inner self, and soulfully directing your path ONLY. What if you were able to just focus on your life, and that entirely? Not aware of what anyone else was doing and experiencing the pressured thoughts as if you were falling behind. Sitting and sifting through where your mind leads and how you can correct your own path through your own actions and decisions not determined by anyone else. What is something you specifically avoid or steer clear from due to the uncomfortable nature? Public speaking? Traveling alone? Staying single for a few years? Where is your comfortability not allowing you to go and how can we break through this barrier for self-growth, overcoming the fear? Are we afraid to disconnect from the virtual world for the fear of not being seen? Accepted by the masses or constant attention when feeling less than at our fingertips? Yet we all crave change and acceptance, so why not make it easier on ourselves to eliminate unnecessary stressors and add new self-guided goals that allow you to transform into someone who believes they are more than enough to diminish the gray areas. As we all have them, but don't voice nor make public. What are these goals and how can we push past the uncomfortable nature of the fear that collides against completing them to propel you forward into what's to come? Not allowing others to dictate your success while leaving it just for your own mental to decide. Stepping away from one world to focus on what's been given to you, altering it in a manner that you have been avoiding or not paying attention to. Eliminating the fear of failure, now that you don't have an audience awaiting the set back. It's for YOU to deal with. Altering different situations in aspects that you would have never found yourself in, if it wasn't for that push of confidence into the vulnerability. Doesn't the saying go, only a few seconds of pure courage can lead to something great? Or something along those lines. Experiencing exponential inner growth excluding the fear of failure, subtracting the constant update of your life to others displaying something unreal, and success in just what is the processes. Learning true, independent transformation through personal growth through only yourself, not only your achievements. Loving, accepting, and absorbing the negative for something greater beyond your knowledge If you were just able to take the first step.

Being comfortable in your discomfort is something I can confidently say everyone struggles with. It wouldn't be uncomfortable if it were easy. As the definition in the dictionary explains. Not one person likes to be pushed to their limits, experiencing emotions that they rather not just to keep hidden in their subconscious for as long as time allows. Through my understanding of life thus far, discomfort is valuable for the possibility of changed circumstance. In the previous chapter, talking about losing direction as I thought I was of mature age to venture out on my own at the age of nineteen, this happens to be a prime example. What I happened to leave out were the mere details that resulted to that decision and what resulted in my return home.

Fired from my first job, right out of school that I thought held the potential to be my career, feeling lost in my life direction, along with the pressure of inadequacy to make something of myself, I decided to make the decision to alter my surroundings. As all my friends were off away at college, perceiving as if they were having a blast, I felt the urge to jump. With only $2,000 in my bank account, I packed my car to the brink and moved solely to Florida from Ohio. Knowing no one, finding a roommate on Craigslist, and getting away from everything and everyone I knew to build my own, new life. Having nothing but pure confidence and the strive for independence. Not so much terrified for the unknown, but eager for this adventure, knowing it was necessary for growth whether successful or not. I had the comfortability of a backup plan, knowing I could always return safely home just resulting with small added embarrassment having to explain my return. But young me was willing to risk the odds and head into the unknown of my future and possible failure. I believed in myself and that's all I needed, minus all the nay sayers repetitively commenting on my possible lack of success and waste of time. Brothers stating, I wasn't mature enough, distant acquaintances calling me insane for the solo journey, and my mother's anxiety projected on me to think of the improbable what ifs. So many opinions, but my mental held strong knowing I was capable of my own success through my individualistic journey laid out. So, that's what I did ignoring the fear of complete failure and destruction. Content with the idea that there was room for mistakes.

Content with barely any furniture in my two-bedroom, two-bathroom apartment located in an upscale town in south Florida, shared with another twenty something girl off the internet, I started my journey. Experiencing all that life had to offer in the unruly state, learning what it took to afford the lifestyle I had laid out. Which consisted of living paycheck to paycheck covering all my bills and just the tiniest bit extra for fun money. It was enticing for a while. Excited to be away from everything and start anew, but that high only lasted if the adrenaline supply in my body. Three months in, I had the lovely experience of running over a nail resulting in a flat tire on my car, noticing it as I ended my workday one random, sunny afternoon. Sitting there alone in the front seat of my car left contemplating what to do. Not having roadside assistance, AAA, or thinking how useful it would have been to of grown up with a coherent father to show me the ropes, concluding I was stuck. Trying to problem solve as my work was closing locking the doors for the day and I was left utterly alone in the parking lot, I had to act quick. I ran back inside the building to see is any of my new coworkers could offer any assistance, which received a reply of eyerolls and excuses to the inconvenience. Dead end there realizing they could have cared less. Next, YouTube…. "How to change a flat tire". Sitting in the lonely parking lot with all the tools I collected from my trunk, trying to follow step by step instructions of a video I found, to only get so far as the third step before realizing I'm not strong enough to loosen the lug nuts. As the familiar car repair shop who rotates my tires had tightened to no end. Pulling, twisting, jumping on the tire iron, I attempted everything possible to lose them…but kept coming up with the same conclusion, nothing.

Before having a complete mental break down, realizing the stream of tears and frustration would get me nowhere, I called my mom. My mom who was 20 hours north of where I sat currently and could do nothing but offer guidance and wisdom over the phone as I had no one. She led me down a list of possible solutions leading me to limping my car to the nearest gas station that was adjacent to my work to ask someone there for help. So that's what I set out to do.

Accelerating as slow as I could not to increase the damage, crossing six lanes of traffic my anxiety had never soared so high. Ending up at the air pump located at the front, highly populated entrance of the gas station to attempt one last hail marry of solutions. Anything I could try the did not result me into having to approach a stranger. Which of course failed, as I thought I could just fill the deflated tire with air to at least get me back to my apartment. Leaving me to the last possible solution to muster up the courage and ask a stranger for help. Sorting through the possible contenders of the gas station, I settled on an older gentleman and his younger son who appeared off first glance like they knew a thing or two about cars. Taking a deep breath, mustering up the courage to approach a stranger for assistance, I started their way. Knowing this could go a multitude of ways, it was my last option. I walked up to pump three and asked in the most kind, helpless voice conveying my desperation for help. The older gentleman smiled with a grin of missing teeth and seemed more than obliged to help as his son stayed in their older ford pick-up. Myself trying to make awkward small talk as we headed toward my car, explaining to the man my situation and him noticing my Ohio plates realizing I was completely out of my element. He confidently replaced the flat in no time, even running into the gas station to buy me a tire gage to carry with me as my car was old enough not to have that feature. He expressed that it was no problem and that he would hope some stranger would attend to his daughter one day, if needed as he did. Warming my heart, he went on his way and me on mine to call my mom and update her on my experience and that I was safe. The worst was over.

I have never been so uncomfortable and vulnerable more any other time in my life than that experience. Which has continued to stick with me to this day. My anxiety levels being pushed to the max out of pure fear and desperation. Leaving a trace of an incident that was out of my control that had the ability to mold me into something new, unplanned. As the universe hand crafted that situation to fall specifically into my lap for whatever changed needed necessary within me to push me out of my designated comfort zone. Considering I would have done anything in my power to of never experienced that level of discomfort and would even avoid reaching out to people, let alone strangers for help. Yet the world said, here you go! This is your lesson! And me having to adapt accordingly, bear in mind I couldn't just sit around and do nothing. Embracing the situation, which was in dire need of action for me to get home. Seeing it as more than just an inconvenience, taking away learned lessons of the position I happened to fall into. Forced to expand my boundaries of strangers and configure how I was going to come out of the situation successful beyond my own understanding and will. As if I had any other choice, again. Seen as, maybe the independence I sought out is something of just that, an image of solidarity rather than something practical. Being young and running off my own endurance and knowledge only got so far being forced to search for an extended hand to solve my issue I wish I could of on my own. Having to step beyond certain boundaries to include someone else, lucky enough to find the kind man and his son. Reflecting on the only person who cared enough for me to end this situation in victory was the person I thought I needed to run from. My role model, my mom. Then resulting in the initial click in my adolescent, not fully formed brain of the possibility that I was the contributing factor to mine and my mother's spiraled relationship. Only to lead to self-reflection for the first time, rather than pointing the finger. I would have never achieved anything if it wasn't for her guidance and the push to muster up the courage to seek help at the gas station. Only for the experience that played out, just so happened to lead me back to what I've always known and who had my best interest at heart. Thinking, if this situation hadn't occurred, where would I have been. If I had been reluctant and listened to my inner stubbornness, how would of the situation panned out. Possibly leading to a very expensive tow truck bill and even further separation from the one who cares most. Resilient to change and that unexpected push but deciding to embrace the unknown for my own benefit considering I've never been in that situation before.

Being uncertain of the outcome of circumstance is more than frightening. Especially for situations that are beyond your control, left for you to fend and navigate on your own. But weirdly enough, I believe that's just life. Once coming to terms that we are not able to control most of what happens to us, welcomes the possibility of acceptance. Acceptance that we are more than what is happening as mentioned prior in my writing, but the way you react and perceive the circumstance determines the view and over all outcomes. A lot of music is inspired by tragedy. Along with movies, art, and other creative successful works. The ability to cultivate that negative emotion into something of great education and self-transformation opens the possibility of being resurrected from what was looked at as a down fall. It's all about perception. Cultivating this new way of looking at circumstance and only projecting your judgement and alterations for the betterment of just yourself. To use as a tool of experience for future times to come. Now, I acknowledge all too well that down falls need to be allowed their time of mourning. To genuinely feel the negative emotions is to live through what's happening. I'm talking about the bounce back. Not being a victim of the vulnerability but acknowledging it to display that it was a momentous situation that cultivated who you are today. That without this forced push from someone greater above or the universe, you would not be their person who looks you back in the mirror today. As these "setbacks" are set ups for what's to come. Like I was supposed to know being in the above situation would have conditioned me to be more open into involving others into my life. Now being able to ask for that helping hand rather than thinking I can take the world on by myself. Winding the road, I paved back to my mother who has been nothing but a positive influence. As explained,

I believe there is a reason behind every experience, positive or negative that can project you into the person you're supposed to be. Learning to channel that energy to achieve that triumph through the uncomfortableness is what conveys your determination. I know I could have used a multitude of examples expressing times where I was uncomfortable and vulnerable, as there are endless circumstances that happened, I wasn't able to avoid, but this one I saw was detrimental for my future self to absorb. Something that corrected the direction I was in from bitter and stubborn to more open and accepting. Allow you mind to explore the times in which you notice the universe change your path via certain situations that would have never cultivated yourself. How do you think they have changed your perspective to this day? For the better, or possible worse and how have they contributed to the outcome of who you stand to be? Being able to accept the situation the way it panned out, alter our reaction, redirecting how we handle similar, future mis-happenings now. It's a formulation of personal, inner growth I've found to help accept the negatives, yet over time transform them into the lesson we unknowingly needed. To be comfortable in the acceptance that things we don't necessarily like happen, and how to use the experience to continue forward.

Concluding my story, a short year later of me living in a different state away from all I've known, I made the final decision to not re-sign my lease and move home to Ohio. Back to my small, cornfield surrounding hometown of neighbors who will be waiting with an array of questions as the new talk of the town. Wanting to get the full details of my independent journey and how it concluded with me settling back to the place I so eagerly wanted to leave. Conjuring up the perfect, repetitive reply to ones who ask, not giving out too much information while also appearing confident in my early return. Unbeknownst to the world, I had maxed out my credit card and had spent all my savings to keep my head afloat while on my own. Living way out of my means, I realized I was over my head and not made for the Florida heat all year round. The move itself wasn't as draining as the constant explanation I had to muster up to repeatedly explain my venture in a way that projected it as a successful learning experience rather than an unfortunate event. Realizing after the fifth consecutive explanation, trying to find the words that fit right into how I wanted to project my journey, the thought of "who the hell cares anyways?" Creeped into my thoughts and morphed what was insecurity to anger. Who were they to say or think anything nearly negative considering I was the one who had the balls to explore the new horizons I sought out? Rather than being ashamed of my what looked like a failure, flipping it into an experience that was able to teach me a multitude of life lessons that this small town would have never urged me to experience. Instead of being afraid of the backlash of a possible negative response from others, I should have just focused on my own accountability and praised myself on all I was able to achieve. Chasing what was my dream at one point, learning it wasn't the path I wanted to take and the universe agreeing. Learning to diminish the opinions of others, not giving them the power to dictate what was my situation. What was my independent journey for my own self growth? The fact that it took me venturing off, states away to acquire knowledge and life lessons for my future self to apply. No one else.

Looking back, I use to think I would have changed a lot about the year explained above. How I would have altered my work ethic and spending habits to project more success to give me the opportunity for what could have been another year in the sunshine state. The type of career I could have pushed more for or downsizing my cost of living or choosing a more affordable area. But honestly, I know things played out the way they were suppose too. Accepting this impulsive decision as a steppingstone of what has made me the person, I am today applying what was accumulated in the unforgettable circumstance I entered myself into. If it weren't for the undoubting self-confidence, accompanied by the ability to push my fear of failure aside, no matter the outcome of this journey there would have been no way I would have found positive in what had played out. I would have never of viewed the daily blessings that I experience now and did before I left, acknowledging now of all I took for granted. Loved ones being so close ready to help, if need be, the familiarity of where I grew up and the surrounding towns, and the constant daily reminder of the person I am today through all I've been through. Once we achieve the ability to find comfort in the uncomfortable, even though a constant cycle as circumstances arises unknowingly, it's how we apply the forsaken knowledge that accompanies the experience that morphs us into someone knew. Growing in the positive and negative.

CHAPTER 7:

OVER COMING
SELF DOUBT

We, as humans tend to be our own worst enemy. Conjuring up negative thoughts and outcomes sourcing from the fear of the unknown. Making assumptions, scaring ourselves from possibilities of our untapped potential, and fueling our own self-doubt. Holding ourselves back from what could be because we feel we are under qualified or inadequate in whatever way. Not even trying for that job we one day wish to have or never talking to that person you find attractive for the over played negative self-talk repeating in your head that is louder than the possibility. I believe it to be naturally our greatest weakness as a species. Could you imagine how easy life would be if there wasn't the constant nag of insecurity? The things you could accomplish and the person you could become would be indefinite, not bound by the ramifications of your own placed lane that you reside in. Forever limiting your own future possibilities. Why is this concept so arbitrary? A life seen as something full of potential rather than an already content path settling, nestled in the comfort. Reaching for experiences, people, jobs whatever it may be that set you on a venture never imaging you would have that you projected out of pure confidence. Seems too easy. As someone who is constantly in their own head, this concept seems like something of a fantasy novel or what God explains Heaven to be like. To walk in pure confidence that who you are and what you are is beyond enough for every situation. Could you even imagine?

As I debate this concept, I realize how much of struggle I seem to have searching for the words that would form this chapter. It has been undoubtedly the hardest for me to write. The others seemed to flow from my brain effortlessly on to the pages. I would escape into the message confidently as something of my past transformed into a lesson revealing a story that has led me to this newfound mindset, I find myself in. While this chapter could not have been the opposite. I wasn't sure as to how or where to start. It seemed this one provided so much trouble as it sat on the back burner for a whole month. Let's be honest, longer than that as I tried to find direction, never confident in whatever opening I created. Not understanding why this concept for me was so difficult to speak on, so of course I waited for the inspiration to hit…hoping it eventually would. Trying to focus on other daily projects than this one, time seemed to pass as I just stared at my unopened laptop dreading the lack of inspiration. Feeling eager to return to conclude my writing project, the inspiration FINALLY projected itself. The idea is in the struggle. What was holding me back and why has creating this chapter been something I wish it would just write itself? Why, so far into this project has this chapter stunted my progress? Diving deeper into the chapter title, it was clear as day. Seeing as I write from experience, authenticity, or triumph over past abuse. The lightbulb finally went off. This concept is something I'm still battling. Overcoming self-doubt has never, nor will ever be my strong suit. How am I supposed to be able to speak on something that I have not accomplished nor even come close to mastering myself and provide direction on how to find comfort in the negative self-talk. Discouraged with my unlikeable start, I found the path once sitting with my own insecurities allowing them to lead me to the root of what was indefinitely holding me back, myself.

The idea that I was attempting to write a book exposing my lack of education and possible life experience to do so haunted me. As I told my stories from my past it seemed if I was journaling and telling my own life story to a group of friends rather than for a piece of work to be possibly published one day. It started to become real that I was a few chapters in, close enough to submit for editing that my anxiety of "is this even good enough" or "do I even have the jurisdiction to attempt this project" overcame me with an accurate flood of self-doubt. Constantly reading back over my work, wondering where I can add more sources and scholars to sight my direction to make my writing credible, it ran me though a constant loop of the possible failure or negative feedback. Like my words or vision weren't enough. I became defeated and scared without even knowing or being conscious of what my thoughts were doing. I was holding myself back from what could be due to the fear of the unknown. The tedious self-doubting finally caught up to the idea of my new project never amounting to anything, that it finally shut the whole production down all together unbeknownst to me that it was my own responsibility. I wasn't giving myself the credit for time and effort I poured into this project I started. Instead, I replayed the negative reality of my situation and frightening myself over it never amounting to anything; staying a simple, saved document on my laptop forever. I was creating my own writers block resulting from my own fear of failure. Once I was able to pinpoint my struggle, I knew I was slowly getting back on track. I knew I found the source and had the power to alter my own reality considering I was the one causing the initial downfall of it all! Making the conscious decision to change the outcome for what I wanted it to be, rather than dreading what it is not currently. I was set to slay the imaginary beast in my mind that I gave so much power too, allowing the project to finally amount to its happy ending. Completion.

Self-doubt is something I struggle with daily. Causing an over abundant amount of anxiety to flow through my whole body creating this ripple effect. As if I just finished running a marathon and the blood is still souring through my veins. The panic of trying to catch my breath resulting from over thinking feels the exact same. Paralyzing me from being the confident, secure woman I so whole heartily strive to be. I over think every small interaction I have with anyone who may crosses my path. Unknowingly, I catch myself conjuring up comments in my mind of how others view me and what they could say, holding myself back from possible self-growth because the fear of wasted time and effort. The weird thing about it; I thought I was the only one who felt this way. Being over stimulated and constantly in their own head. I never opened and when I did it was always to the wrong people. Resulting in misunderstandings or never being able to receive the correct sympathy or comfort leading me to shut down more due to the constant miscommunications. As if I was always too much. Perceived as if I constantly over-reacted to all situations, big and small. Little did I know, it was the people I surrounded myself with that also contributed to this thought pattern. I continued to create my own crippling anxiety that convinced me that everyone only saw the bad, along with surrounding by myself with the wrong people it was a recipe for utter failure. My chapped lips, my lack of education, my loud laugh; Basically, everything negative that I MYSELF believe to be my worst qualities replayed constantly in my mind as if the insecurity was displayed on my forehead projecting onto other people. Causing me to stunt my own personal growth without even realizing it and projecting nothing of the less about myself. Before understanding that I was my own worst enemy, I didn't understand why my life felt so complicated all the time. As if every day there were new mental battles that I needed to overcome which felt EXHAUSTING. I thought to myself, "if this is the real world, then I don't want it". Never officially contemplating the idea of suicide, which is the extreme, but to the point where I viewed life as pointless because all it felt like was a constant, never-ending avalanche of stress. That my life was full of dread and uncomfortable situations. Not wanting to get out of bed to deal with the everyday battles I felt like I was facing alone. Turning to who I thought were friends and my support system only leading me further down my rabbit hole I created. But I had to work my 9 to 5, pay my bills, and be an active part of society to push myself though. I knew this couldn't be it for me.

Enough became enough when I felt like I was faking the smile for far too long. Everything felt empty and staged. As if I wasn't in my own body and just accepting my life for what it was, not knowing I was in control. Posting pictures online as if everything was okay, receiving compliments back easing that dark feeling with a temporary high that lasted 3 seconds. Hanging with friends exposing only the bare minimum finally matching the energy they provided accepting this relationship was as deep as it gets. Finally starting to consider the possibility of the positives of changing my inner circle after keeping everyone at a distance, being absurdly nervous to express myself due to their lack of their support. This as if all 7,830,458,560 people on this planet matched what they selectively offered. Which lead me to looking for solutions of how can I help myself and where should I even start? I don't like this life and what can I do to make it the exact opposite of what I'm living? Because clearly my daily happiness wasn't going to come from anyone other than myself and whatever I'm doing now is not the correct formula. The process had to start and end with me. Attempting to reach out and find positive solutions to cope, I started my search. Knowing that these feelings I've battled for a while don't just magically go away, yet something to be worked on and something of progression, not perfection. All I needed was to start. Start somewhere and keep going.

I started with my appearance. Specifically, for myself, I knew I always felt so much better when I was actively working out and focus on a healthy lifestyle in general. As I found eating as a coping mechanism that didn't have the best outcome. I would look forward to eating something that was so wrong for my nutrition but tasted oh so right! It would release that small projection of serotonin that felt so foreign to my mind leading me wanting more. Finally realizing that temporary feeling of what tasted good would only go so far. Looking at myself in the mirror, hating the reflection I knew this is something I could control with a little self-discipline. Thinking, I always worked out and tried to be healthier when I was in high school, playing sports and always onto the next activity, so I don't think it would be so difficult to slide right back to it?! I mean, I was that person one time or another, I can get her back. The adult version of myself after high school would always plan to start a new regimen, but then fail once achieving that goal thinking it was a one-time progression rather than a lifestyle change. Or even going for a run and rewarding myself with two honey buns diminishing all my hard work, thinking it "balanced out". Resulting in me gaining all the weight back just to reside at square one. Confused as to why I wasn't getting my results, I had to recalibrate. I started to dive into cooking and finding healthy alternatives for the food I ever so craved without starving myself or beating myself up overeating a cupcake. Pinterest became my best friend until I got the hang of healthy meal-preps. Weirdly enough, a year later, broccoli is my favorite food and almost even contemplated going vegan. And if you knew me, I was always the girl getting the double meat portion in every meal possible. It was something that made me feel confident and I was excited to tell people about my new love for healthy eating as I never knew it was possible to live this way. Yes, I became one of those people. But the positive effects it had on my body made me want to share it with others, exposing this super easy way to flood your body of natural serotonin. I never shied away when being offered a cookie because I know I have configured a new self-control. If I wanted chips, portion control was my best friend baby. A diet change doesn't mean skipping out on all your favorite foods. It just means everything in moderation with a high focus on what is good for your body! Learning to eat with the result to nourish my body instead of seeking happiness due to the action of feeling full, I altered my mind set to still enjoy food, but also for the result of a longer satisfaction going beyond taste. A longer, healthier, happier life living as me.

Combined with my newly redefined diet, I found a workout routine that transformed my body even though it's a workout I swore I would never do. I became a runner. Hating every second of the tiresome mile I forced myself to run a day, muscles started to form in places I didn't even know I had. My legs became lean, my stomach flatter, and after that dreaded 10 minutes, I would call it quits, never able to endure more. But somehow, that was enough for my body as constancy and creating the habit are key! I just kept doing it unsure if this new workout routine would give me the results I wanted or not, I just tried something different. Forcing myself to be uncomfortable for my own growth, eventually leading me to the results I sought out. My parents reluctantly had a treadmill as I never was able to muster the courage to run in front of people at my hometown gym, or any gym in that matter. I looked awkward, had a heavy foot, and felt like pole would just gawk at my lack of stamina and overly projected sweat glands leaving me soaked from just a mile jog. I knew starting in private was best for me mentally. Allowing the journey to be my own, going at my own pace instead of focusing on what others might possibly be thinking of my inexperience. Starting slow from a pattern of run – walk – run, I was able to start slowly jogging the whole mile in a less than brag-able time. But I finished and that's all that mattered. The slow combination walk/jog miles turned into a constant pace, leading into a shorter mile time as time progressed and my body's speed and stamina increased. Mainly wanting to stay active for my mental well-being, I started to notice a universal change throughout the life I was living. A body I could be satisfied with, not disgusted or shameful of, the extra burst of energy I felt through the day, and the feeling of constant accomplishment rather than self-pity from the lack of daily activities. Knowing I was the one enforcing the change and not feeding the lazy, bad habits I acquired. The healthy alternatives I found myself in started a chain reaction of, well, if doing something different has already push me this far, how far can I take the new lifestyle? Leading into my sense of style; going from t-shirts and leggings to bright colored, tight dresses, and skirts. Wearing things, I would have sworn off years ago, completely chaining my own self-image. Evolving into this new person, full of potential who has been waiting to be shown off, but never had the means to convey.

Now, for starters, my path and your constructed path look absolutely nothing alike. Our upbringings are different, the people I surrounded myself with are different, and the choices I have made are just of my own. What has worked for me could have been something you have tossed out the window from lack of results, and that's okay! The whole idea is to try something so out of reach that your old self would think you're crazy for even trying. Being able to muster up the confidence and motivation to kick start new habits is half the battle. Including the will to even notice the bad habits present and starting the journey to reevaluate where you can tweak them for personal growth. It's not about shaming who you are now, it's about making yourself better. I truly believe our souls were made to accumulate knowledge and transition throughout life due to circumstance. In my opinion, we are never meant to stay the same. The mindset you had in high school will only get you so far in your early twenties and your young adult life can only get you so far into your mature adulthood. There's a time for everything (Ecclesiastes 3:11) including change as well. Notice when habits that are no longer serving you a higher purpose in your life. Accumulate an idea of who you wish to be and begin a step at a time into the right direction. There's no room for self-doubt because you aren't even sure of this new person you are searching to be. This is a journey of self-improvement, and any inconsistencies or negative attributes are brought to the table solely by yourself, making them super easy to turn off. Giving others no jurisdiction to make comments, judge you, or misconstrued who you are as you are metemohpiesizng into the new you! You're creating your cocoon baby; just wait for the day you can confidently break free and show off your wings!

CHAPTER 8:

LET'S WRAP THIS UP!

I've talked a lot about myself and my own weird journey on how I've become the person I am today. Not sure if I'm even doing this "life" thing the right way but having the best intentions for myself and others seems to be the best way to go! It's all about becoming the best version of yourself and not getting stuck in that dark, gloomy hole of the same old that we find ourselves in, trying to portray different online. With social media, it has been easier than ever to hide the truth. Not showing the whole situation, rather just the new and braggadocios events that the universe blesses us with hiding the trials and tribulations of what it took mentally and physically to get to that point. This never-ending road of ups and downs becomes manageable when we obtain a clear vision of who we want to be, always guiding our next steps into possibility when we stay true to our inner selves. Respecting the process and embracing the changes of your current situation. Meaning, everyone is always in the time of transition, yet what we do with that time makes the difference. Rather than trying to uphold a false narrative online, being able to dive deep into who you are and exploring the endless possibilities of self-induced change is the true goal of life. Forever moving, changing, and altering the person you have found yourself to be for the better. Taking the negative connotation out of the saying "you've changed" rather receiving it as a compliment.

Truth be told, everyone on this abundant green earth has no idea what they are doing, and life is forever throwing you into a transition altering the ideal straight path you sought out, exchanging into an endeavored rollercoaster of hills and obstacles to conquer. So, the only mindset that really matters is your own! Your life, your path and at the end of the day it's your own opinion that shapes your outlived reality. No amount of likes on a picture or number of followers determine the specialty of whatever you have achieved or the insurmountable devastation you might have faced along the way. Your journey starts and ends with you and hopefully by the end of this reading you have been able to navigate and find the true self that has been patiently waiting in the background. The man or woman behind the phone so effortlessly scrolling for a new reality. Hopefully one day achieving the everyday goal of living the life you want, rather to please others or show off any sort of status. Being confident and secure in the person you choose to be and live out a life base off your sole opinion of happiness. You only get one life baby, why are you trying to live it according to someone else's plan, or society's guidelines? Make your own and use it as the guiding map to never end success sought through your own personal perspective!

To be happy with who you are seems like such an unobtainable goal sometimes. Something out of reach or unrealistic due to the fact of the influence in our day and age. As if there's always something better out there. Whether it be clothes, your living situation, or any form of relationship. We always see life with 'the grass is greener on the other side' mentality. Especially now with the edited versions we share on our devises, it's easy to look at others and place them automatically into a better situation as to what you're currently in. I mean, the daily routine now is to wake up, check for notifications. You're awkwardly standing in line at Costco by yourself? Check the feed. It's a constant go to that we have all incorporated into our daily routine for comfort and constant connection. Yet, how much abundant false data has your brain downloaded all out of convenience. Seeing friends on vacation while you're at the store doing normal things that everyone does. A quick reminder of the daily grind you have fallen into as we age. The NORMAL routine we all create for ourselves to live comfortably, while we view others on the beach...graduating...getting married. Quite frankly what seems like the exact opposite of what's happening in our lives. Appearing to be more successful than you, considering you're just buying milk and they are pictured sipping mimosas on the beach. To break the news to you.... everyone is shielding the norm from being exposed, whether they admit it or not to seem less inadequate! So, let's cut the BS of picturing everyone's lives greater than our own and focusing that energy into creating a life with the sole purpose of making ourselves happy and satisfied. We have no idea what was happening behind the scenes of those pictures. How many times they had to repose to get the right angle. So, the whole visual for that matter is what we solely make of it. Creating our own narrative yet needing to learn how to expose the falsifying details that are left to our own minds to form, filling in the blanks. Learning to find comfort and beauty in the norm of our everyday. Romanticizing buying that milk, just to come home to warm welcoming family. Exercising the convince and privilege to afford milk that is so outrageously priced now a-days. Finding blessings in the same old and shove out the noise that says whatever you are doing currently is not flashy enough. As I rant on and on about something I must remind myself constantly, allow me to put this final chapter more into an understandable perspective that I found to be a great realization. Involving a life lesson, I have had the joy of obtaining recently by the universe.

The wonderful and forever entertaining Netflix is constantly releasing a wide range of documentaries that pique my interest and can keep me engaged until the very end. How? With my attention span? I have no idea, but I recently came across an informational series that showed the lives of multiple famous singers that displayed their journey of stardom through their personal experience rather than the only edited documentary highs and lows yet nothing in-between. You see them post on all social media platforms throughout their career, you hear their music, you wish to meet them, yet a different narrative is playing out behind all the publicity we are subject to. As they are being controlled by their labels to be this strangely elevated figured rather than a real person. Because you know, they are just regular people too lol. Unknown depression, insecurities, dropped labels and so much exposed during these binge worthies' series reveal the reality of these idolized, relatable humans. SO much we would have never imagined going on behind the scenes, yet it did, and we're updated of the true journey after the fact. After the judgements, after the awards, after the ridicule of what was their talent and perseverance to be successfully climbing the social ladder of a harsh reality. Only portraying this fake persona to the masses and us mindlessly believing that we knew this character. Not seeing the man/women behind the flashy media. Until documentaries are shown giving them a platform to display the real side of their experiences. Behind just the music produced exposing the reality of their day-to-day struggle to become a success. Humanizing these public figures as if they were our own neighbors and not someone who acquired success I could only dream of. Demolishing the thought of these celebrity lives being an untouchable force, breaking down the barrier of our own selfish ideas of who we think they are. Characters stripped down revealing nothing more than humans who indulged their wanted purpose to the fullest creating this new persona. Editing their life for what was needed to attract the masses for success, shielding us from the whole picture to acquire more attention. Leaving out the important struggle that came along the way. While they were able to edit what was seen to the world, mentally and individually is a different story. Not being able to skip the unimaginable hurdles it took to obtain the fame and fortune, but finally being able to express what it took to become that character. They were able to play up this image so much that their own personal needs were lost in translation leading to other outlets like drugs, alcohol, and a long list of mental health issues now suffering the repercussions of pursuing their false self they created all these years. They changed their whole life for the fame, future, and material success that their psyche of who they were has now been altered to believe those are the concepts that define their self-worth. Everyone loved Hannah Montana, but did they love Miley too? Sorry, had to use my generational reference. Whether these people displayed themselves as their character or their true self, only one of them was really waking up and going to sleep with them every night. Yet they gave so much to the narrative persona, allowing the media to portray them as one way, when we, as viewers have no idea who we are really idealizing.

What impeded me to explain this series was the amount of determination for a better situation each of these individuals had that once started out as a hobby, then a dream, morphed into their new reality from self-motivation. Focused on manifesting the path they could obtain rather than comparing inadequacies to already accomplished individuals. Never fearing the start of possibility with a mind of negativity or wasted time. Could you imagine the possibilities of placing all the wishing, wanting, and waiting energy of your dreams into untapped potential? Seeing how your life could be and having impeccable determination to get there. It just starts and ends with you. Acquiring vision of where we see ourselves and how we could get there. Something I do every year as I see changes in my own personal life, I write down where I want to be. Financially, in my relationships, career, and over all self-wellness. I get a vision, and I start there as many of these other famous men and women did. Now my dream isn't to preform ion stage in front of millions of people. To me that seems like a panic attack just waiting to happen. But what about financial stability? What about acquiring new, secure relationships with family members? Or making time for myself for self-improvement?

Writing things down or even making a vision board of how you see your life improving by only your definition. Cutting out the comparison of all others distinct paths to completely alter your own! I'm all for reviving inspiration of what could be from others, maybe someone lives in your dream house, has your dream family or job. But that doesn't mean it isn't obtainable in yours. Sulking in battles, or your current situation shouldn't be the focus. Possibility should. We have so much power to change our situation, it's just possessing the right mind set to achieve what is sought out.

This journey of life is only yours and no one will experience it the way you are. No one feels your emotions or knows your motives behind why you do. Why even try to explain? Believe that you can live a better life than the one currently and start taking the self-empowered steps to achieve it for your own embitterment and not status. Start doing actives for the love of the activity and not the great post it would provide content for. I can't express enough how much power everyone on this planet must completely flip the situation they are currently in. Your sole purpose of living should not be to impress everyone else. Yet to find the things we hold value to and indulge! Due to all the mental roadblocks, it seems impossible, yet coming from a woman who is now in the conclusion chapter of her book, who RARELY picked up a book through school. If you don't believe in yourself, on who you are and who could be, how can you expect others too? We all want to be present, understood, and listened too, but if you don't like the voice speaking, where does that lead? Nowhere!! Changes in your circumstance start with you and the energy you allow in. Shut out the clutter of the out-side world, opinions, and rules. Talk to your inner voice and attract what feels right and allow it to consume your new every day. You dictate your own future…. let's see what you have in store next!

SOURCES CITED:

1. https://psychology.wikia.org/wiki/True_self_and_false_self

2. https://www.simplypsychology.org/psychoanalysis.html

3. https://weinholds.org/how-the-false-self-gets-created/.

4. https://www.cdc.gov/nchs/products/databriefs/db362.htm

5. https://my.clevelandclinic.org/health/articles/12942-fostering-a-positive-self-image

6. Cohen–Swerdlik • Psychological Testing and Assessment: An Introduction to Tests and Measurement, Seventh Edition

7. Daring Greatly: How the Courage to Be Vulnerable Transforms the Way We Live, Love, Parent, and Lead – Brene Brown